about *Speak with Courage*

"Reading *Speak with Courage* was like listening to my favorite professor lecturing." — Elizabeth Robertson Hornsby, *Southeastern Louisiana University*

"Public speaking was always a source of fear to me. Thanks to *Speak with Courage*, I feel more confident than ever." — Anna Pettus, *student*

"As a beginning speaker, the book *Speak with Courage* left me feeling as though my nervousness and fear of the lectern was normal, and it served as a fantastic vehicle for adapting to those fears by becoming self-aware." — Rick Marren, *student*

"*Speak with Courage* integrates the research of communication studies scholars, combines it with insights from other disciplines and the popular press, and frames its strategies with common sense and practical wisdom." — Dr. Isa N. Engleberg, *professor emerita, Prince George's Community College, and past president, National Communication Association*

SPEAK

WITH

COURAGE

50+ Insider Strategies for
Presenting with Confidence

Martin McDermott
Brookdale Community College

Bedford/St. Martin's
Boston ◆ New York

For Bedford/St. Martin's

Publisher for Communication: Erika Gutierrez
Senior Executive Editor for College Success: Simon Glick
Developmental Editor: Lori Cerreto
Editorial Assistant: Catherine Burgess
Senior Production Editor: Ryan Sullivan
Assistant Production Manager: Joe Ford
Marketing Manager: Stacey Propps
Copy Editor: Hilly van Loon
Indexer: Melanie Belkin
Art Director: Lucy Krikorian
Text Design: Meryl Levavi
Cover Art and Design: Billy Boardman
Composition: Jouve
Printing and Binding: RR Donnelley and Sons

President, Bedford/St. Martin's: Denise B. Wydra
Director of Development: Erica T. Appel
Director of Marketing: Karen R. Soeltz
Production Director: Susan W. Brown
Director of Rights and Permissions: Hilary Newman

Manufactured in the United States of America.

8 7 6 5 4 3
f e d c b a

For information, write: Bedford/St. Martin's, 75 Arlington Street, Boston, MA 02116
(617-399-4000)

ISBN 978-1-4576-3834-3

ABOUT THE AUTHOR

Martin McDermott is Associate Professor of Speech Communication at Brookdale Community College in Lincroft, New Jersey. A graduate of Rutgers University, he pursued graduate studies at Ohio State University, and was awarded a Distinguished Scholar Fellowship at the University of California, Santa Barbara, where he earned a master's degree in Communication Studies. Martin has taught more than 3,700 students during his tenure at several colleges and universities, grading over

15,000 presentations in the process—and counting. An active member of the National Communication Association (NCA), Eastern Communication Association (ECA), and New Jersey Communication Association (NJCA), he also conducts continuing education workshops and coaches speakers of all levels in support of their personal and professional goals. A native of Trenton, New Jersey—with family roots stretching back to Brazil, Italy, England, and Ireland—he enjoys travel, film, songwriting, athletics, and learning about a broad range of subjects. For more information about Martin McDermott's training and coaching services, please visit **www.martinmcdermott.com**.

PREFACE

WHEN I BUMP INTO FORMER STUDENTS — WHICH HAP-pens more frequently the longer I teach — they seem to recall three things about public speaking class: how nervous they initially felt, the topics they spoke about, and the joy of gaining confidence over the term. Like before-and-after snapshots of a physical fitness program, they are proud of their hard-earned speech muscles. Course content, however, is a different matter. Inductive reasoning? Monroe's Motivated Sequence? Argumentum ad populum? Often a distant blur.

Given that fear of public address is one of the most viru-lent of human anxieties, this highlight-reel retrospective of speech class makes sense. Students recall milestones. One might summarize the speech student's journey by paraphrasing Julius Caesar's triumphant report to the Roman senate after routing in one afternoon the army of an ill-prepared enemy: "I came. I spoke. I conquered." All else is just commentary.

Whether teaching college, corporate, or community educa-tion classes, I've been struck by one simple fact: Actors, teachers, doctors, lawyers, college deans, college students, CEOs, entertainers, combat veterans, and even psychotherapists—they all get scared on the podium.

Numerous studies confirm this finding. Most recently, Karen Kangas Dwyer and Marlina M. Davidson of the University of Nebraska–Omaha replicated the often-quoted 1973 Bruskin survey, which popularized the notion that people fear public speaking more than death. The results? Rather than 41 percent of respondents choosing "speaking before a group" as their most common fear, 62 percent of the 2,543 college students who participated in the study identified public speaking as such—a 21 percent increase over the Bruskin survey.[1] Death ranked as the third most common fear among students.

Things just don't have to be this way. Whether you've never spoken in public or have done so a hundred times, anyone can present with joy and confidence. Whether young, seasoned, bold, shy, male, female, student, or executive, this book can help. *Speak with Courage* distills nearly two decades of field-tested ideas into fifty-six user-friendly strategies for overcoming speech anxiety. Each chapter reveals powerful answers to the same pivotal question: What mental or physical choices can you make to put yourself at ease as a speaker? The answers you learn will forever change how you see, prepare for, and give presentations.

Let's now look at seven key features of *Speak with Courage* that lay the foundation for this quantum shift. These features will help students, general readers, and also instructors who want to integrate the book into their course lesson plans:

---

[1]Karen Kangas Dwyer and Marlina M. Davidson, "Is Public Speaking Really More Feared Than Death?" *Communication Research Reports* 29, no. 2 (2012).

1) Speak with Courage *offers a wide variety of strategies for managing speech anxiety.* We are not a one-size-fits-all species; neither should there be a one-size-fits-all solution for speech anxiety. Whatever the slant, each chapter shares a common goal: to help readers speak from a place of strength and courage. Everyone has a different way of reaching that place, so the book offers dozens of starting points for this important journey.

2) Speak with Courage *combats communication apprehension during all phases of the speechmaking process.* From thinking about your first speech (Section I) to basic speaking strategies (Section II) to moving past fear (Section III) to selecting content (Section IV) to stepping onto the podium (Section V) and, finally, to analyzing one's performance after a speech (Section VI), the book offers practical guidance on how to make fear work for you every step of the way.

3) Speak with Courage *offers sound instruction on many key elements of public address.* A speaker selects, shapes, arranges, recalls, and presents ideas to a group. With its easy-to-follow chronological format (Sections I to VI), the book walks readers down each avenue of their speaking adventure *as* it unfolds. Rounding out the speaker's journey, "The Big Picture" (Section VII) explores broad perspectives that cast a wider light on public speaking. A resourceful instructor can easily teach the skill of public address with this text alone!

4) *Many of the book's fifty-six strategies promote rhetorical competence in any communication setting, not just at the lectern.* Whether interpersonal, small group, business, or public communication, speaking up with greater confidence, clarity, and power will serve every reader's academic, personal, and professional goals.

5) *The style of the book is conversational and its tone warm.* While the scholarship is solid, with relevant sources noted, the book invites learners to read for pleasure rather than study as a rote chore. Chapters are brief so that students quickly find help. Chapters are varied to reflect the diverse backgrounds and temperaments of students. Chapters are engaging so that students enjoy learning. Don't be misled by the brevity of the book's chapters; they are brief in the reading but powerful in the doing.

6) *A correlation chart conveniently maps out the book's pedagogical content.* By cross-referencing *Speak with Courage* with topics covered in a traditional public speaking course, both students and instructors can easily dovetail class content with readings from the book.

7) *End-of-section summaries and "Points to Ponder" reinforce core ideas and help readers apply the strategies from each chapter.* Readers will welcome these exercises as a series of stepping-stones that lead from the page to the podium. Instructors can rely on these 142 prompts for classroom and online discussions or assign them as written exercises. (For learners who prefer a digital format, *Speak with Courage* is also available as an affordable e-book that includes all of the above features.)

Underpinning this structure, the unique purpose of *Speak with Courage* makes it a one-of-a-kind book. *Speak with Courage* addresses the unspoken concerns of students head-on. Fear is the elephant in the speech classroom, and the book wrestles this elephant to its knees by both tusks. Although a major concern for *most* speakers, *most* public speaking textbooks fail to devote even a single chapter to the topic. Many include just a few pages. Unlike this cursory handling, the comprehensive treatment of speech anxiety in *Speak with Courage* mirrors the actual magnitude of student fears. This distinction is critical. For if we communication experts are doing right by our students, how is it that millions of Americans dread public speaking *after* successfully completing public speaking courses?

Off the podium and beyond the classroom, *Speak with Courage* continues to offer tremendous value. Dr. James C. McCroskey's prolific research established "communication apprehension" as a debilitating factor in all human interactions, whether face-to-face, in groups, or in formal presentations.[2] This makes sense. Whether we sit, stand, or face a camera, we still *present* ideas to an audience. And whenever there is a message to share, there is often an anxious communicator. The book's strategies will help learners to speak with greater confidence at any time and in any place.

During my more than 7,000 hours in the classroom, I've watched too many young men and women suffer needlessly while trying to express themselves. I wrote *Speak with Courage* out of compassion for these students. While some seasoned professionals may have forgotten that tossed-into-the-deep-end terror that engulfs a novice speaker, students haven't. Students want someone to toss them a life ring. Floodwaters nip at their noses, and even the finest instruction book on swimming does little good if the reader remains afraid of the water. If a speech book inadequately addresses the fear of speaking, it likewise misses the mark.

Despite its emotional challenges, public speaking is not like performing neurosurgery or an Olympic balance beam routine. You don't need a lengthy apprenticeship. It is not a black art

---

[2]James C. McCroskey, *An Introduction to Rhetorical Communication*, 4th ed. (Englewood Cliffs, NJ: Prentice-Hall, 1982).

passed from Hogwarts School of Witchcraft and Wizardry professors to eager sorcerers-in-waiting. Our students have been standing on their feet talking since they were toddlers. From their lifelong exposure to classrooms and the media, they carry thousands of templates for effective speaking in their mental Rolodexes. Fear gets in the way. It's that simple.

Speak with Courage addresses this central and perennial student concern. The book offers calm, friendly, and reassuring guidance for the vital adult challenge of public speaking. Like a trusted speech-coach-in-a-book, its pages will soothe jangled nerves while simultaneously helping students to craft content. As one student-reader commented, "*Speak with Courage* will leave you wondering why you ever feared public address."[3] While the book offers many starting points for this life-altering journey, its sole and unequivocal end is to unlock the speaking potential of your students, students whose voices will one day echo throughout our communities, nation, and, for some, around the world.

Acknowledgments

No worthy book takes final shape without assistance from many hands. My deepest gratitude is owed to two very special aides-de-camp: Ann Van Hise, whose devotion to the book has outlasted all others, and former student Dr. Sandra K. Cruz, who was, during the book's gestation period, a patient and gentle muse. My heartfelt gratitude also extends to Sheila Levine for her sage and cheerful counsel, to Dr. Isa N. Engleberg for her generous support, to Dr. Kathleen Williams for her enthusiastic adoption of the text in her honors speech classes, and to

---

[3]Jamie Pullen, e-mail to author, July 7, 2011.

Brookdale Community College for a sabbatical that framed the initial version of the book.

Working with a publishing company that develops authors and deeply values the beauty and power of the printed word has been a joy, and many dedicated employees at Bedford/St. Martin's deserve recognition. I must first thank Joan Feinberg and Tom Scotty, co-presidents of Macmillan Higher Education, along with Denise Wydra, President of Bedford/St. Martin's. Driven by persistent belief in the book's value, Publisher Erika Gutierrez and Senior Executive Editor Simon Glick started and sustained the momentum that was needed to complete this worthwhile project. My special thanks go out to Lori Cerreto, Developmental Editor, and Catherine Burgess, Editorial Assistant, who guided this book through many rounds of editing and revising.

Others at Bedford/St. Martin's who made invaluable contributions include Lucy Krikorian, Art Director; Joe Ford, Assistant Production Manager; and Shuli Traub, Managing Editor, who all kept this book running on its fast-paced schedule. I appreciate the sharp eye Associate Production Editor Kellan Cummings brought to his initial work on this book, along with the good humor and sound judgment of Senior Production Editor Ryan Sullivan, which helped to shepherd this project to an idyllic close. Additionally I must thank copy editor Hilly van Loon for her commitment during this entire project. It is important to recognize that this book would not have been able to reach any student without the dedication and enthusiasm of Stacey Propps, Marketing Manager of Communication; Sally Constable, Senior Market Development Manager; Shelby Disario, Manager of Promotions and Advertising; Pelle Cass, Senior Designer; and Sara Hillman, Senior Designer. Senior Designer Billy Boardman has my deep gratitude for his cover design and original illustration.

I am also indebted to the many kind student and faculty reviewers who provided valuable feedback on all aspects of the book, including Shae Adkins, Lone Star College–North Harris; Ray Bell, Calhoun Community College; Mardia Bishop, University of Illinois at Urbana-Champaign; Benjamin J. Cline, New Mexico University; Michelle B. Coleman, Clark State Community College; Neva Kay Gronert, Arapahoe Community College; Christine Kelso Holland, University of North Florida; Emily Holler, Kennesaw State University; Elizabeth Robertson Hornsby, Southeastern Louisiana University; Richard G. Jones Jr., Eastern Illinois University; Susan Kilgard, Anne Arundel Community College; Steven J. Madden, Coastal Carolina University; Jodie D. Mandel, College of Southern Nevada; Holly Manning, Laramie County Community College; Lynn Meade, University of Arkansas; Rebecca Mikesell, University of Scranton; and David D. Moser, Butler County Community College.

Finally, to the thousands of public-speaking students whose struggles and triumphs are reflected in these pages, I applaud your bravery. You have accomplished what many fear to do.

CONTENTS

III. Cognitive Strategies   55

IV. Managing Content   95

I

Opening Vistas

1

Fear of Public Speaking Is Commonplace

MICHAEL KEARNEY GRADUATED FROM SANTA ROSA Junior College at age eight. At fourteen, he earned a master's degree in biochemistry from Middle Tennessee State University. At seventeen, he began teaching at Vanderbilt University. When lecturing on the topic of argumentation, I jokingly challenge students and ask why they haven't yet received their own master's degrees. They are at least eighteen years old and have taken community college classes, so what's the holdup? Students quickly point out my faulty reasoning: I've jumped to a conclusion; I've made a hasty generalization. I haven't provided enough evidence to support the claim and my lone example is atypical—Michael Kearney is a genius with an IQ over 300. He is an exception to the rule.

In another telling way, public-speaking students believe they are all too much like Michael Kearney. They, too, are exceptions to the rule. While assuming that speechmaking is a breeze for the rest of the world, many students believe they suffer like no one else on earth. Perhaps it's the depth of their anxiety, its duration, or the torment of repeatedly lying awake at 4:00 A.M. with a speech looming ahead, but some students insist that the speech gods descended from Mt. Olympus and personally cursed them.

Let's test out this argument. First off, how common are phobias, the irrational and often exaggerated fears that haunt human beings? The *Diagnostic and Statistical Manual of Mental Disorders* (DSM-5), the psychotherapist's "Bible," states that "it is common for individuals to have multiple specific phobias" and that many burdened with such fears have "changed their living circumstances in ways designed to avoid the phobic object or situation."[1] The more common maladies make the rounds as household names: acrophobia, the fear of heights; claustrophobia, the fear of enclosed spaces; agoraphobia, the fear of open areas; and arachnophobia, the fear of spiders. But that's just a start: over ninety phobias populate in-depth lists.

Next, how common is the fear of public speaking itself? The often-quoted *Bruskin Report* (No. 53) ranked this fear, called glossophobia, at number one, above the fear of death. *The Book of Lists* did the same. A 2007 survey of British supervisors ranked public speaking as their most dreaded task. A large percentage of Australians in a 2008 survey feared public speaking more than death. And on this side of the pond, researchers estimate that up to 85 percent of Americans experience anxiety when faced with giving a presentation. With a current population of over 315 million, roughly 270 million people in the United States will fear standing at the lectern.[2] Sign your membership card on the dotted line and welcome to the club; you just might not be able to find a front-row seat.

Hopefully, you will breathe easier knowing that the gods haven't smitten you with a case of speech anxiety that is unparalleled in human history. The scarlet *A* of anxiety is not stitched on your sweater. No telltale neon sign flashes above your head. If anything, anxiety may be the price that our entire species pays for the gift of speech. If so, what shame is there in experiencing the fullness of your own humanity?

While gazing across this broad new vista, let yourself relax a bit. Unclench your fists. Take a deep breath. Look around. You're in good company. The fear of public speaking is as common as fingers and toes. Taking constructive steps to ease it, however, is not. That is what the rest of this book is about. The good news about phobias is that we can outgrow them. Anyone can leave behind the fear of public speaking, if they wish. You will not be an exception to that rule—I promise.

2

Even the Famous Get Scared

I F "ALL THE WORLD'S A STAGE," AS SHAKESPEARE WROTE, then many people must be frightened. In the field of speech communication, we keep pace with studies that document stage fright, take note of famous accounts in textbooks and the popular press, and witness firsthand the struggles of our own students. At times we share stories to bolster a class's flagging confidence. Tales of the rich and famous trembling in the spotlight—of squeamish actors, royalty, and rock stars—evoke a keen fascination.

Consider these telling anecdotes: Thomas Jefferson so dreaded public speaking that in his eight years as president he gave only two major addresses. James Earl Jones, the deep, rumbling voice of Darth Vader in *Star Wars* and Mufasa in *The Lion King*, stuttered so badly as a teen that he refused to speak outside his home. And Barbra Streisand, after a self-imposed, twenty-seven-year exile from live performances, only appears with the aid of a teleprompter that displays every spoken word and belted-out lyric of her stage act. Actor Harrison Ford summed it up best for many when he described his speech at an awards ceremony as "a mixed bag of terror and anxiety."

If this opening whets your appetite, I've assembled a representative group of over sixty skittish notables here for you, a veritable *Who's Who of Stage Fright*. Their cases are documented by journalists, biographers, and historians — outed by the press, if you will. Some luminaries you have read about; others you've heard rumors about. Some lived hundreds of years ago, some live now; some are old, some are young. Some struggled with stage fright through a period in their lives; some struggled throughout their entire lives. Whatever your generation, you will recognize a number of these marquee names.

Although your curiosity might now be piqued, I don't want to evoke the atmosphere of a carnival sideshow, so let's airbrush the scene a bit. Before reading the list, imagine that you've just visited the Museum of Tolerance in Los Angeles, California, or the Vietnam Veterans Memorial in Washington, D.C. Hold that feeling of reverence in your heart. Now, imagine these names chiseled into a set of sleek black granite panels in front of you. You stand before this monument under a gray sky, your reflection casting itself into each polished slab of stone.

Read through our roll call one name at a time. Don't rush. Each person might have something to tell you. Rest on a marble bench and reflect, and then stroll around the grounds for a while. After you finish, we'll meet on the other side of the iron gates.

Adele • Lucille Ball • Kim Basinger • Beyoncé • Warren Buffett • Richard Burton • Johnny Carson • Johnny Cash • Cesar Chavez • Cher • Winston Churchill • Cicero • Marie Curie • Charles Darwin • Leonardo DiCaprio • Michael Douglas • Thomas Edison • Albert Einstein • Gloria Estefan • Ella Fitzgerald • Jane

Fonda • Harrison Ford • Mahatma Gandhi • Judy Garland • Billy Graham • Hugh Grant • Daryl Hannah • Billie Holiday • Jennifer Hudson • Thomas Jefferson • Scarlett Johansson • James Earl Jones • Nicole Kidman • Kris Kristofferson • Jay Leno • Abraham Lincoln • Shirley MacLaine • Madonna • Marilyn Monroe • Van Morrison • Conan O'Brien • Sir Laurence Olivier • Donny Osmond • Al Pacino • Luciano Pavarotti • Joaquin Phoenix • Natalie Portman • Elvis Presley • Chris Rock • Eleanor Roosevelt • J. K. Rowling • Charles Schwab • Carly Simon • James Stewart • Harriet Beecher Stowe • Meryl Streep • Barbra Streisand • Lily Tomlin • Randy Travis • Ritchie Valens • Oprah Winfrey

A moment of silence, please. No snickers. As poet John Donne wrote, "Never send to know for whom the bell tolls; it tolls for thee." If you struggle against the grip of speech anxiety, this is the company you keep — a pretty impressive group.

I hope you noticed two things as you read through the list of names. First, no one on our roster became so famous, so powerful, or so talented that he or she ceased to be human. Even those who command legions of fans or followers contend with the Achilles' heel of their own humanity. Next, I hope you see the list as a living memorial, not a graveyard. All have flourished in spite of fear. All have succeeded in creating worthwhile lives — we wouldn't be reading their names if they hadn't. The fear of public performances did not steal the dreams or fire from any of these hearts.

Our brief tour is now over and the monument is about to close. What will you do next? I hope you will keep these kindred spirits in mind whenever you face the fear of public speaking. Although afraid of the limelight, they have lived and worked in it. Perhaps their courage will inspire you. Each notable was driven into the public arena by a love of his or her calling, not by a love of the spotlight. Our world would be less without their risk-taking. And perhaps you will also remember that no amount of money, fame, power, talent, or beauty gets you a free pass. The playing field is even. No gods stand upon stages or speaking platforms. Any speaker can bleed, so even the famous get scared, just like you.

3

Great Fear Can Precede Great Growth

JENNIFER WILBANKS'S WEDDING DAY DIDN'T TURN OUT as planned. Instead of a honeymoon in the Caribbean, the Georgia bride-to-be ended up on a forlorn stretch of Route 66 in New Mexico, seemingly the victim of a kidnapping and assault. Her frantic 911 call alerted police about her alleged abduction, which took place three days earlier while jogging in an Atlanta suburb. The truth was a bit more complex. Jennifer tossed away her own jogging clothes, cut a few inches off her long hair, and used the Greyhound ticket she had purchased a week earlier to escape the pressures of her impending marriage. Cold feet turned this thirty-two-year-old nurse into a runaway bride, triggering a nationwide missing person search and leaving her fiancé, fourteen bridesmaids, and six hundred wedding guests in the lurch.

Rites of passage can evoke great anxiety for anyone. Other milestones that provoke sleepless nights include the first day of school, going away to summer camp, prom night, the first day of a new job, buying a home, starting a new business, the birth of a child, and retirement. Public speaking is also a rite of passage. We go from being a face in the crowd to *facing* a crowd. We go from standing in the audience to *standing up to* an audience. The magnitude of this challenge can make anyone want to turn and run. In fact, in each school at which I've taught, dozens of students sign up for a public speaking course each term and then fail to show up for any of the classes — just registering for the course is all some students can handle at first.

This reluctance to even set foot in the classroom suggests the course's unique power. While important, subjects such as statistics, biochemistry, or business law probably won't turn you into a different person. Public speaking can. Students can't sit in the corner and hide during speech class. Like life, participation is required. An instructor says, "Stand up; let's hear what you have to say." After twelve years of sitting in rows, raising a hand to speak, and watching teachers commandeer the classroom, the request to take center stage can trigger great distress for some learners. The journey from their seats to the front of the room is a long one for many students.

Those who march on and complete public-address coursework pass by two important mile markers. First, public speaking as a skill set opens up pathways to many new careers. Among these professions are law, teaching, politics, public relations, advertising, sales, consulting, training, and media work. Students often feel excited when they realize these new choices. "I didn't think I could speak in public," they will tell me, beaming with satisfaction after a solid first speech. Second, since public speaking is the greatest fear of many people, a tremendous surge in self-confidence arises when we confront it. This great growth spurt, this movement from childhood to adulthood, can occur even long after our physical bone ends have closed.

In the early 1970s, psychologists popularized the term "comfort zone." The farther past the edges of your comfort zone that public speaking lies, the greater the growth you will experience. While many students feel sorry for their classmates who experience high levels of speech anxiety, the fearful are sometimes the most fortunate in class. Ironically, students who fear the most will grow the most. Like a first glimpse at shooting stars on a moonless summer night, these learners will encounter mind-broadening vistas that their more self-assured peers may never see.

This very prospect of great growth can produce great fear. If you are bigger than you previously assumed, life might then expect bigger things from you. Like the metamorphosis from caterpillar to cocoon to butterfly, unexpected new possibilities emerge. The person that you were before, afraid to face a crowd, is no more. A larger, more capable person has taken his or her place. Author Marianne Williamson poetically captured this quantum shift in the following passage from her book *A Return to Love*:

> Our deepest fear is not that we are inadequate. Our deepest fear is that we are powerful beyond measure. It is our light, not our darkness, that most frightens us. We ask ourselves, Who am I to be brilliant, gorgeous, talented, fabulous? Actually, who are you *not* to be? You are a child of God. Your playing small doesn't serve the world. There's nothing enlightened about shrinking so that other people won't feel insecure around you. We are all meant to shine, as children do.[3]

Whatever our age, we were all once children, and we were all once students. Seeing the world as a classroom without walls, we are all still children, and we are all still students. Don't run from your lessons. Walk towards growth; don't sidestep it. Learn to accept fear as an engraved invitation to growth. The greater the fear, the higher you must rise to overcome it. Taken in this spirit, standing up to speak—even on cold feet—will add several inches to your height.

4

Indulge Your Self-Interest

IF DOG-EARED COPIES OF *THE ART OF THE DEAL* BY DONALD Trump and *Think and Grow Rich* by Napoleon Hill sit side by side on your nightstand, this technique is for you. Some of the strategies in *Speak with Courage* suggest altruism, but here's a chapter for those who believe that the Salvation Army bucket is for suckers. I'll give you three reasons based on pure self-interest to overcome your fear of public speaking. Don't worry if Mother Teresa is more of a hero to you than Bill Gates, one of the richest billionaires on the planet—you'll still want to absorb these key reasons for conquering speech anxiety. They just might inspire you to new heights that will make your mama proud.

First, think about your career advancement. Did you know that public speaking is a skill in great demand by Fortune 500 companies? Each year the National Association of Colleges and Employers surveys blue-chip companies and ferrets out the qualifications these top employers covet in new hires. According to its *Job Outlook 2012*, verbal communication ranked as one of the most sought-after skills — again. In today's tumultuous employment arena, public speaking skills may not only get your foot in the revolving door for a first job, they may also keep you gliding up the corporate staircase as you advance within and between companies.

Second, we are all smitten with skilled public speakers. Since most people fear giving presentations, the public speaker is a bona fide daredevil. In fact, Gallup's December 1999 poll of the most admired people of the twentieth century includes Billy Graham, Ronald Reagan, Winston Churchill, Eleanor Roosevelt, and Nelson Mandela — all fine speakers.[4] As this list suggests, speakers are also seen as leaders. Well-established research on group dynamics tells us that those who speak early and often typically emerge as leaders of the pack. On a grander scale, Barack Obama's speaking prowess no doubt factored into his back-to-back presidential victories. Even on the college campus, looks, brawn, and GPA take a back-row seat to eloquence in the classroom. You don't kick sand in the face of the skinny collegian who can speak. Whether in school, running for public office, promoting your own business, or being called upon to give a eulogy or wedding toast, your time on the soapbox can pay handsome dividends.

Third, for those who like big paychecks, it might surprise you that public speaking, hour for hour, is one of the highest-paid professions in the world. In 2007, for example, business tycoon Donald Trump spoke at the Learning Annex's Real Estate Wealth Expo and earned $1.5 million for each one-hour seminar that he presented. Annualizing his speaker's fees tallies up to a salary of over $3 billion a year. The highest-grossing speaker on record, however, is former president Bill Clinton, who earned $31 million in speaker's fees between 2001 and 2005 alone, according to the *Washington Post*. While President

Clinton touts the most gilded tongue on the speaking tour, other presenters command stratospheric fees as well. At the time of this writing, Billy Crystal, Ellen DeGeneres, Dr. Oz, and—hold your horses—Larry the Cable Guy all command over $200,000 per speaking engagement.

In summary, to get the fast-track job, the adoration of the crowd, and the exorbitant presenter's fees, public speaking is a powerful gadget to slip into your self-promoter's toolkit. Given the possible professional, social, and financial rewards, can you really afford to be afraid of the podium? The "me first" message here is clear: To get ahead, leave behind the fear of public speaking.

Before I unleash you on the world, a last-minute confession is in order. As a teacher, I hope that your gas tank runs on more than high-octane self-interest. But if these reasons are what it takes to motivate you, I'm willing to meet you on the street where you live. Research and common sense tell us, however, that those who live and work while keeping others in mind are happier. So, after you make your millions and jet off to lunch meetings with Bill Gates and Warren Buffett, remember to give back to the poor huddled masses, like these gentlemen and the Salvation Army do.

5

Big Brother Isn't Watching You

IN GEORGE ORWELL'S ONCE-FUTURISTIC NOVEL *1984*, BIG Brother keeps an omnipresent eye on the comings and goings of all citizens. Other than store security monitors and the vigilant antiterrorist surveillance cameras on street corners in cities such as New York and London, most inhabitants of earth come and go with little notice. The truth is, your own big brother might not want to keep an eye on you, let alone some worldwide security apparatus.

Many speakers nonetheless drag a suffocating hyperawareness with them to the lectern, imagining that *every* audience member is aware of *every* thought, breath, and bead of sweat that rises from them. This is a far cry from the truth. While we experience ourselves in three dimensions with Dolby Surround Sound, to an audience a presenter appears in two dimensions on a flat screen. Private thoughts create added temptations for listeners. Whether pierced by Cupid's arrows or making mental to-do lists, we daydream on average "up to half of our waking hours," according to psychologist Eric Klinger, author of the seminal book *Daydreaming.* Never mind fretting over audience members tracking you with the precision of laser-guided radar; a speaker's first task is often just getting a crowd to pay attention.

To further compound matters, human beings are naturally egocentric. As Irish playwright Oscar Wilde once quipped, "To love oneself is the beginning of a lifelong romance." Why would this love affair end when you are on the podium? While we are the stars of our own dramas, audience members, for the most part, remain preoccupied with their own affairs. If there is something in it for them, they listen; if not, well, you get the picture. Here's another perspective on the human condition: This is how I experience MY LIFE; this is how I experience your life. This is how I want you to experience ME. It sounds crass, but if it weren't true, nary a hungry or homeless person would roam this earth.

Dimming down the hot stage spotlights is a relief for some speakers, for others a disappointment. If we fancy ourselves so important that everyone should notice everything about us all the time, like film stars hounded by frenzied paparazzi, we will be disappointed. This naïve expectation is a holdover from childhood. Perhaps our parents came to the school play, music recital, or championship game with cameras in tow, but other adults have other priorities. I feel bad for students who bring soaring hopes with them to the lectern. On a warm spring day, during an afternoon class, towards the end of the term, their classmates might struggle to pay attention. Despite my responsibility to grade student presentations, even I occasionally lose focus after hearing six hours of speeches during back-to-back classes.

If there is a silver lining to these cloudy thoughts, realize that much of speech anxiety is a private rather than public drama. The tremors in your hand, rumble in your gut, swoosh of arterial blood, helter-skelter thoughts, and sickening dread of rejection flicker off the audience's radar screen. The bittersweet reality of public speaking is that no one will watch or remember your talk as keenly as you. You are the principal witness to all your speaking deeds.

Despite this fact, many speakers assume that audiences will notice every minor performance flaw, because these errors seem so painfully self-evident to a speaker who is standing at the lectern. While we experience ourselves from the inside looking out, audiences size us up from the outside looking in. Because of our privileged vantage point, we can be our own harshest critics. I often notice this when teaching. Even talented students will lament how poorly they've done after a truly fine speech, assuming they have failed the assignment, and then confess a litany of trivial errors that I didn't notice or deem important.

To keep things in perspective, realize that human attention is not an unforgiving laser beam; it comes and goes in gentle, well-rounded waves. This is more good news. When you stand up to speak, relax. There is no eye in the sky. Breathe freely. Big Brother isn't watching. Connect with yourself. Connect with your material. Connect with those who listen. Speak your piece. Plant a few seeds. Speak to give something to your audience, even if they don't always give back the attention you want or deserve. After the rain falls, flowers may still bloom between the sidewalk cracks.

6

All Survive, None Perish

Each day, millions of people around the world give speeches. Think about it. The United States alone boasts nearly 4,200 colleges and universities. Most of these schools conduct speech classes. At Brookdale Community College, for example, over 1,200 students take public speaking each term. Business professionals also roll out presentation after presentation after presentation. If you had Superman's X-ray vision and could peer through buildings in New York, Tokyo, Caracas, or any other large city, you would witness hundreds of simultaneous presentations. And then there are political speeches. Our world has nearly 200 countries, each with municipal and state-level government officials who each day report on their work, react to unfolding events, and campaign for office. Encouraging our spiritual aspirations, religious leaders in every nation speak in mosques, temples, churches, and synagogues — day in and day out.

The world resounds with speeches. We just can't see or hear them all, but they are there. If we could magically walk down the corridors of history and listen to the past, millions more could be heard. And the miraculous thing? Everyone survives. Despite the strength of our fears, we don't switch on the news to hear, "Dozens more perish during speeches, details at eleven." It just doesn't happen. Heart disease, cancer, and car accidents—these are the big culprits, not speeches.

As a novice instructor many years ago, I worried about what might happen on speech day in my classes. Like you, I heard that terrible things happen when people speak in public. I even memorized the phone number of the campus police in case we needed an ambulance. Since that time, I've heard more than 3,500 students give over 15,000 presentations. Have any of them ever fainted? No. Have any of them ever vomited? No. Has any student even felt dizzy? No.

All speakers, past or present, go through the same process. They find out they have to speak; they feel nervous. They prepare; they feel nervous. They stand up to speak; they still feel nervous. They sit down, and they live to tell the tale. The score? Public Speakers: 375,000,000; Death: 0.

Make dinner plans. You will live to tell your tale, too.

II

Basic Strategies

7

Let Fear Energize You

ALL ACROSS THE ANCIENT WORLD, ALCHEMISTS STRUGGLED to turn base substances such as lead and cinnabar into gold. These early scientists dreamt of transmuting crude, common elements into ones much more rare and precious. In the emotional realm, many speakers carry within them something just as ordinary and abundant—fear. Is there possibly an alchemy for speakers, a magical process to transform the humble emotion of fear into something of greater value?

The popular author and motivational speaker Tony Robbins challenges us to ask some unorthodox questions when facing a predicament: "What's good about it?" or "What could be good about it?" Robbins uses a cognitive technique called "reframing"—the same painting hung in a new frame creates a fresh impression. So, let's ask: What's good about fear? Does fear hold something of value for you as a presenter? How might a savvy speaker use nervousness before, during, or after his or her talk?

The answers seem strikingly clear. You need energy to do research; fear provides that energy. You need energy to rehearse;

fear gives you that energy. You need energy to deliver your speech; fear supplies that energy. Rather than shrinking you down, fear can fuel great vocal and physical animation and enlarge your presence as a speaker. After a speech, fear will also motivate you to learn about and correct mistakes. When illuminated in this kinder light, fear softens and steps out from the shadows as an unexpected ally.

Fear only becomes a problem when we try to force it away. If you believe that you shouldn't feel afraid, you will suffer from both the fear itself and your violated expectation. Sixteenth-century French essayist Michel de Montaigne put it this way: "He who fears he will suffer, already suffers because of his fears." Take Montaigne's advice. Don't fight fear. It's just raw energy. Harness it. Throw a saddle on top of it. Use it in your service. If fear awakens you at 4:00 A.M. on the morning of a speech, check your notes, rehearse a bit, and then go out for a brisk walk or run. If you feel maddeningly nervous days or weeks ahead of a talk, go way over the top during a half-dozen or so rehearsals to release that pent-up energy. Let fear propel rather than hinder your speaking journey. A Zen Buddhist saying captures the essence of this simple strategy: "It's easier to ride the bull in the direction that it's going."

Although fear is a very powerful emotion, a surprising thing happens when you let it energize you. Before long the fear that stymied you will transform itself into genuine excitement. Because emotions are quicksilver impulses—like clouds that shift during strong winds—if we let them run their course, they simply dissipate. The worst strategy is to stiffen up and try to tamp down all that nervous energy. I've seen my share of macho presenters, both male and female, who straightjacket their bodies and voices because they are so afraid to look afraid. Like imploding stars, these rigid speakers lack the radiant energy needed to touch or inspire an audience.

Some of the world's largest waves pound the north shore of Oahu, an island in the state of Hawaii. Experienced surfers paddle out and ride fifty-foot waves back to shore unharmed. Only the skill level of the surfer creates limitations, not the size of the wave. A big wave is simply a big opportunity for a seasoned surfer. Riding the wave of fear is like surfing. Rather than getting thrown off the board, experience will teach you how to skillfully pilot the swells and tsunamis of fear. The more skilled you become, the more thrilling the ride. One day you will look forward to the excitement of "surfing" and forget that you are even speaking. Waves of emotion will still energize you, but any ripples of fear will grow smaller and farther apart.

8

Think of Public Speaking
as a Conversation

SOMETIMES I JOKE AROUND IN SPEECH CLASS, STRIKE A dramatic pose, and with my best highbrow British accent blurt out, "But soft! What light through yonder window *seeps*?" The class laughs. The famous quote from Shakespeare's *Romeo and Juliet* is, of course, "But soft! What light through yonder window *breaks*?" Students laugh at my antics because they recall the line, word for word, from high school English.

Many speakers stagger under the weighty assumption that a speech is just like a play: Every word, gesture, and movement must be crafted in advance and committed to memory. Speakers imagine that they begin with a perfect score of 100 and lose points for each deviation from the divinely preordained structure of their speech. This is nonsense. Speeches entail preparation, an audience, and perhaps even a stage, but they are unlike theatrical performances in many important ways.

Here are six key differences: First, there is no need to memorize most speeches. Ancient Greek and Roman orators such as Demosthenes and Cicero spoke for hours without notes.

Nowadays, Herculean feats of memory are out the window. A simple outline with key words and key phrases is an acceptable memory aid.

Second, unless you are a CEO or head of state, you don't need a manuscript for a speech. World markets and world peace don't hang in the balance if you misspeak, and quotes from your talk won't festoon the front page of the *New York Times*. Relax; forgoing a manuscript actually makes your job easier. A keyword outline requires less writing, allows for greater flexibility, and invites less criticism since listeners can't compare your spoken remarks to a word-for-word draft of your speech.

Third, although speeches can entertain, most often your goal will be to inform or persuade. Forget about your sketchy *Saturday Night Live* routine. Public speaking is not stand-up comedy. Many speakers stir hearts and minds without evoking sidesplitting laughter. Watch any politician on C-SPAN for a sobering reminder.

Fourth, you are free to be yourself when speaking in public. Actors, on the other hand, mimic the vocal and physical mannerisms of the characters they portray on stage or on screen. Oscar winner Robert De Niro, for example, gained sixty pounds in four months to play the aging boxer Jake LaMotta in *Raging Bull.* Preparing for theatrical roles can be tedious and time-consuming; being yourself requires no added effort.

Fifth, while there is *no* room for deviation in staged performances, extemporaneous speech allows for greater flexibility. The nearly 9,000 performances of *The Phantom of the Opera* have all been the same. Whether July or December and whether 600 or 1,600 patrons fill the theater, the play runs two hours and thirty minutes with one intermission. Each song lyric and line of dialogue remains unchanged. While top-notch, lockstep performances sell tickets for Broadway shows, orators can ad-lib, forget material, and even stammer a bit, yet still do an effective job.

Finally, when performing a play, actors don't typically take their cues from the audience. Some even erect a "fourth wall" between themselves and theater patrons to shut out the world beyond the stage. By contrast, sensing audience reactions is vital during a speech. If you see boredom or question marks on the faces of audience members, you can alter your pacing or content to meet their needs. This difference is crucial. Theatergoers *witness* an event; speech audience members *participate* in and shape an event. Although a Broadway show is set in stone after the opening curtain and might flop within a few weeks, a speaker can alter his or her remarks on the fly for a more favorable outcome. In this sense, audience feedback helps "direct" you towards a winning effort.

With these distinctions in mind, realize that a speech is more like a conversation with a friend than a theatrical performance. If a buddy called and asked for five minutes of your time to hear about a topic you know well, say cooking or snowboarding, would you fret and lose sleep over it? Would you say, "Call me back in a week; I need to rehearse"? No, you'd happily share the information. So why stress over a presentation? Haven't you been standing on your feet talking since you were two years old? Just do the needed research, structure a talk with a few main points, rehearse a bit, and then share your ideas.

Bam! Serve up a great speech.

9

Prepare, Prepare, Prepare

HUMAN BEINGS PUT OFF WHAT THEY DON'T LIKE DOING. Dental checkups, tax preparation, retirement planning, and speech writing huddle in the same shunned corner of the room. Not surprisingly, humans are least prepared for some of the most important duties of their lives. According to *Consumer Reports*, for example, about two-thirds of Americans die without a will.[1] Even notables such as Abraham Lincoln, Howard Hughes, Karl Marx, and Pablo Picasso died intestate. There is a key difference, however, when procrastination affects public speaking: Your failure will be public, not private. While no one knows if tartar engulfs your teeth as you munch on a donut in the break room, messing up a presentation gives coworkers something to talk about around the office watercooler. If not for the joy of excellence, then the fear of public humiliation should goad you into adequate speech preparation.

Speech preparation has three distinct yet interrelated aspects: cognitive, physical, and emotional. Cognitive preparation entails conducting research on your topic, selecting the best ideas possible, and effectively organizing your thoughts. Physical preparation simply means rehearsing your presentation. The first attempt at a speech should never be in front of a live audience on the due date. Working without a net is for circus acts only. Finally, like an advanced storm-warning system, emotional preparation gauges and plans for the strong feelings that might arise while speaking, with fear being chief among these.

You might compare the three steps of speech preparation to asking someone out on a date. For your best shot with Cupid, you come up with something catchy to say, rehearse it a few times, and then anticipate possible outcomes. Forgetting your heartfelt lines or getting caught flat-footed by an unexpected no or yes can spell disaster. After all, what if your intended really does have a root canal scheduled for Saturday? Plan for possible surprises, and remember that speech preparation in one aspect invariably affects the others. Solid content, for example, generates confidence, which will then improve vocal and physical delivery.

Inadequate preparation creates predictable problems. Totally unprepared speakers who throw themselves on the mercy of the crowd fare the worst. When students dutifully show up in my class and speak without preparation, it's like watching a deer in the headlights of an oncoming tractor trailer in slow motion. Both speaker and audience feel grueling pain. Other speakers do research and construct fine outlines but never practice. They tend to go over or under the time limit, forget key points, have ragged transitions, mispronounce unfamiliar words and names, or get blindsided by unexpected waves of anxiety. For these unprepared speakers dog-paddling on high seas, the outline or slideshow bobs like an irresistible life ring, and they resort to public *reading* when they should engage in public *speaking*. Without the experience of a live practice session, other speakers get what I call "rapture of the podium." "Wow, I'm up here and all these people are listening to me. This is really cool. That reminds me of another story. . . ." Wake the audience when the love affair is over.

On a more serious note, students who put off assignments until the last minute sometimes opt for the easy way out. Plagiarism has swelled to epidemic proportions in American education. According to anonymous student surveys conducted by Dr. Donald McCabe of Rutgers University, a national expert on cheating in U.S. schools, 95 percent of high school students admit to cutting ethical corners sometime during their education. The numbers for college students aren't much better.[2] A different *p* word lies at the root of plagiarism: *procrastination*. Sadly, I've heard my share of pirated Internet articles, doctored to look like outlines at 3:00 A.M., passed off as original speeches. By stealing ideas, these students fail both themselves and the assignment. Undergraduates, however, haven't cornered the market on intellectual theft. Allegations of plagiarism have cast shadows over the careers of author Alex Haley, film director James Cameron, *New York Times* reporter Jayson Blair, and even Vice President Joseph Biden. Adults get to wear the dunce cap, too.

In case you've lost count, I intentionally left the thesaurus on the bookshelf for this chapter, and some variation of the word *prepare* appears thirty times in four pages. Make it your mantra. Om. Shanti. Prepare. You don't have any control over the weather, the stock market, or the audience, but you certainly do control how well you prepare. The not-so-subliminal message here: Being prepared will reduce your anxiety and increase the likelihood of a positive outcome. So do your homework, then relax. Preparing for success will breed success.

In review, prepare your mind by selecting the ideas and words of your talk, prepare your voice and body by rehearsing the delivery of your speech, and prepare your heart by anticipating the waves of emotions that accompany public speaking. Inadequate preparation often leads to a self-fulfilling prophecy: Fearful speakers who underprepare do poorly and then fear public speaking even more. Your fate is in your own hands. A successful speech is not a matter of luck; it's a matter of preparation. Legendary film producer Samuel Goldwyn summed it up best: "The harder I work, the luckier I get." The three morals of this story: Prepare, prepare, prepare.

10

Ask for a Little Help

W E COME INTO THIS WORLD TETHERED TO AN UMBILI-
cal cord. For nine months before birth and for many
years afterwards, our survival depends on the goodwill of others. Although cute and cuddly, we can't sit, crawl, stand, walk, or
speak—neither can we feed, wash, or clothe ourselves. Changing our own diapers is out of the question. Human beings, in
fact, have the longest infancy of all mammals. By the time we
reach puberty, the family dog has already matured, mated, raised
a few litters, and passed on.

Our apprenticeship is lengthy because living in a human culture is complicated. Other mammals don't drive cars, perform
calculus, or give presentations. Regarding the latter task, public
speaking is a complex skill set. A competent speaker must select
and research a topic, choose and organize ideas, draft an outline,
construct visual aids, hold rehearsal sessions, retrieve large
chunks of information from memory, clearly articulate each
spoken point, master the rudiments of physical and vocal delivery, and continually read and respond to a live audience—all

while keeping speech anxiety in check. No wonder presenters get nervous; that's a lot of plates to keep spinning!

Asking for help can turn the above to-do list into a do-it-together list. Why not call on a friend to test out your arguments, help with pronunciations, time your speech, check over your outfit, pass out handouts, advance your slides, hold up objects, smile when you speak, flash secret timing signals, be the first to clap, be the first to ask a question, take you to lunch after a talk, let you vent, or share kindhearted feedback when the stage lights dim? With an open mind, only your imagination and the help you're willing to ask for will limit what you receive.

Let's take this one step further. Why reinvent the wheel? Or, in the case of speechmaking, the entire wagon? If you've been graced with drive and organizational skills, why not assemble a support *team* around you? Ask a friend who can write well for outlining help. Ask an artistic colleague for guidance with visual aids. Invite your bubbling-over-with-bright-ideas buddy for a brainstorming session. With today's global communications networks, you can text, tweet, and Facebook your way into recruiting a virtual team. "Many hands make for light work," as declared by a time-honored English proverb.

Academic research on small-group decision making shows that, when tackling complex problems, groups make better choices than individuals left on their own.[3] So, in addition to the camaraderie, working with a small group before a presentation can yield sizable payoffs. If you do collaborate with others before stepping onto the podium, you will follow in some rather large footsteps. In *White House Ghosts: Presidents and Their Speechwriters*, Robert Schlesinger reveals that every U.S. president since 1920, except Calvin Coolidge, has worked with full-time speechwriters. Consequently, some of the most famous lines spoken in presidential speeches—such as Ronald

Reagan's "Mr. Gorbachev, tear down this wall!"—were hammered out on a collective anvil.

For some, tearing down inner walls and reaching out for help can be difficult. The more vexing or difficult a task is, the more some of us tend to adopt an "I'll show you" mentality and go it alone. Crumpled papers, softly lit by a computer screen, ring the wastebasket at 2:00 A.M. History provides an attitude adjustment. During a presidential campaign speech on October 22, 1928, Herbert Hoover declared that "rugged individualism" spurred both the American citizen and nation on a relentless "march of progress." He believed that government aid to citizens and intervention in business should be kept minimal for maximum economic growth. One year after Hoover's speech, the stock market crashed and the Great Depression crippled America. Millions were left jobless and homeless. Rolling up our collective sleeves and working together put a staggering nation back on its feet. Interdependence, not independence, describes the human condition. Unless you build your own home, grow your own food, generate your own power, and clear your own roads, others make your daily journey possible.

We come into this world knowing and owning nothing. Perhaps we leave the same way. During the intervening journey, after the umbilical cord to our mother is severed, much good flows to us through others. On the grand stage of life, someone already possesses or can point to whatever you need or want. On the small stage before you, someone who crosses your path may have the exact ideas, advice, or support that you need for a presentation. Although you will stand alone in the spotlight when you speak, much of the behind-the-scenes work can be accomplished beforehand with others. In other words, don't be afraid to ask for help. Knock hard. You never know how wide the door will open.

11

Hold Dress Rehearsals

FEW NOTEWORTHY PUBLIC PERFORMANCES ARE STAGED without practice sessions. Plays, parades, concerts, musicals, and even weddings require rehearsals. Along other lines, winning sports teams practice their playbooks, civil authorities run disaster drills, and militaries around the world hold live training exercises. Even the president of the United States practices the State of the Union Address — rehearsal is not beneath his pay grade.

Practicing in front of a live audience is critical for your speaking success. Why? How will you handle stage fright if you've never or only rarely felt it? Dress rehearsals pump up your adrenaline level and give you a chance to navigate the unpredictable tides of anxiety. You can also get a feel for the timing of your speech, iron out some of its rough spots, and receive valuable feedback from practice session volunteers.

Who should be in your practice audience? Anyone with ears and a pulse, anyone who will listen — friends, neighbors, relatives, coworkers, classmates, your kid brother, the cocker spaniel, and if you're stuck late at the office, the night cleaning crew. Give them chocolate. Promise them backrubs. Name your firstborn after the one who claps the most. Anything if they will listen. These kind souls might save you from failure and humiliation. As written in the Book of Hebrews, "Thereby some have entertained angels unawares." Given their importance, however, don't test out the first scribbled draft of a speech on a volunteer audience; work from a decent outline to build your confidence and receive on-target feedback.

The most successful students tell me their in-class speeches were the tip of the iceberg; they practiced many times beforehand. By contrast, the least successful students tell me, "I should have listened to you, Professor McDermott! I didn't practice." If you avoid dress rehearsals because you're too nervous, I can promise a speech doesn't get any easier on the due date. Why wait for the cameras to roll? Get the mistakes out of the way during a dry run. When you do face your audience at the appointed hour, you'll feel more relaxed and confident knowing that your speech has already passed muster.

As famed football coach Vince Lombardi observed, "The only place where success comes before work is in the dictionary." So, five, six, seven, eight—once more with feeling! Run it by the practice squad until you get it right.

12

Familiarize Yourself with the Speech Setting

My FIRST DAY OF TEACHING COLLEGE WAS A DISASTER. About five minutes into my opening remarks the lights went off in the classroom. No light slipped in past the steel door or cinder-block walls, so the room was pitch black. After an awkward silence, all twenty-seven students erupted into laughter. I froze. A young man from the college basketball team finally fumbled his way along a wall and switched on the light timer. When the cool fluorescent lights flared up again I felt the redness spreading across my face. This was the first public speaking class that I taught—not a warm welcome to "Teaching 101."

I made a rookie mistake that day by not checking out the room before I taught. If I had, I would have noticed the unusual light dial. Other teachers knew about them. In fact, each term more experienced graduate teaching assistants at Ohio State University pranked their junior colleagues by sneaking into lecture rooms between classes and setting the light timer to five or ten minutes. In my case, ignorance was not bliss.

Three good reasons should motivate you to inspect the location where you will speak. First, by familiarizing yourself with the setting, you can avoid mishaps like the one I experienced. Knowing about room size, room brightness, light switches, projectors, ambient noise, computer equipment, seating or table arrangements, and whether there's a chalkboard, whiteboard, or flipchart will assist with your preparations. During a pre-speech visit you might also discover that the lectern is missing or notice blinding sunlight if the curtains are left open. Better to spot these hazards before rather than during a presentation. Also, ask yourself how things look from the audience's perspective when visiting a room. Are views obstructed? Are the seats comfortable? Can you sit for a lengthy spell without squirming? Devise plans to address any room limitations.

Second, in addition to tackling practical matters such as whether you should tote along chalk or dry-erase markers, making the room your own gives you a psychological edge. In professional sports the home court or home field advantage is well known. A thirty-year study of America's Major League Baseball from 1977 to 2008 showed that home teams won 54 percent of the games played in their ballparks.[4] Even world championship teams with stellar records fall in defeat more often on the road. The roaring home crowd lifts team spirits, no doubt, but familiarity with home turf also makes play execution easier.

So, when possible, practice in the room where you will present. Walk up and down the aisles and then saunter around the room's perimeter. Sit in a few chairs and check out the view. Make it your own turf. Feel a bit of swagger, like you're walking down the street you grew up on. When the audience arrives they're stepping into *your* neighborhood. You've already sat in their seats and filled the room with your voice. You're in charge here.

Finally, knowing the setting of a speech might help you shape its content. Talks and speeches should never be generic, one-size-fits-all productions. Each talk is for a particular audience in a particular setting on a particular occasion. Speakers sometimes refer to the actual setting during a speech. These references adorn commemorative addresses such as commencement and dedication ceremonies. During the Gettysburg Address, for example, President Abraham Lincoln said, "We are met on a great battlefield of that war," then mentioned how fallen Civil War soldiers had already consecrated the ground on which living audience members then stood. Without awareness of the setting, obvious or sublime speaking opportunities might pass you by.

In summary, human beings often fear the unknown. Limit the unpredictable by checking out the setting of your talk. This familiarity provides both a practical and psychological edge, and a greater level of comfort will lead to a greater level of performance. Along those same lines, show up early on the day you present. Something might have changed since your first visit. Double-check the equipment. Make sure everything works okay. Move the chairs around if crowding or blocked views present a problem. Then breathe and relax. Greet people warmly as they arrive. They are now entering your house.

13

Have a Backup Plan

WOULD YOU GO SKYDIVING WITHOUT A RESERVE PARA-chute? Would you go rock climbing without ropes and a harness? Would you swim the English Channel without a support vessel? Surprisingly, many folks engage in public speaking—an activity more feared than any of the above—without a backup plan. As in the rest of life, the unexpected can blindside you at the lectern, and a crowd primed for a speaker after an enticing introduction doesn't want to hear, "Where do I put my flash drive?" as the opening line.

Difficulties during a speech can feel like tumbling towards earth in free fall, so anticipating them in advance will make for a softer landing. A few years back, I spoke at a community college outreach conference attended by high school administrators. I had tested my slideshow on the computer the day before, but after being introduced as a speaker, my PowerPoint file wouldn't open. Several hundred educators watched. Not to worry—being familiar with the room, I projected printouts of my slides through a document camera so the audience could follow along. No one was the wiser.

As this story suggests, knowledge of often overlooked details can mean success or failure during a speech. Predicting all problems in advance is impossible, but crafting general backup plans along with specific strategies tailored to your unique speaking situation is time well spent. Alternate game plans will help you in several ways: You will feel more confident, you will be able to handle problems if they do arise, and you might even discover better ways of presenting your ideas while pondering plan B. The more you think in your seat, the less you need to think on your feet.

The risks of public speaking lie in your unique rhetorical circumstances. Every speaker must grapple with a specific audience, occasion, setting, and topic. Unscripted dramas triggered by tardy handouts, broken equipment, upended speaking schedules, and fickle public address systems can upstage you. As you consider these and other relevant variables, imagine some worst-case scenarios for your talk. How would you handle each? Mentally rehearse your emergency plans in case you need to grope for the rip cord and deploy the backup chute.

Along with a plan for anticipating problems unique to your speaking situation, let's review six common challenges and their easy solutions. Seasoned speakers routinely face these predicaments and you can benefit from their collective wisdom.

First, the computer doesn't work. Always bring a hard copy of notes or slides so you have an outline to speak from. A savvy speaker will bring along his or her own laptop as a primary or backup system.

Second, the microphone won't work. Walk up and down the aisles and hold court like a coach during a championship game. Before the introduction of electronic public address systems in 1915, presenters always relied on old-fashioned lung power.

Third, the projector conks out. Steady your hand and write on the chalkboard, whiteboard, or flipchart. If you brought a copy of your slides, which you should have, walk down the aisles and let audience members glance at these printouts while you speak.

Fourth, there is no microphone and loud noise from a nearby room or roadway outside drowns you out. Speak louder, move closer to audience members, and send out an emissary who can negotiate an end to the disruptive noise. As a last resort, move the group to a quieter location, if available.

Fifth, audience members arrive late because of traffic jams or other meetings, delaying the start of your presentation. Don't panic. Mix and mingle with the crowd. A few minutes of schmoozing might provide added insight into the audience, which will then boost your influence as a speaker.

Sixth, your speaking time is cut down. If you speak last on a program with many presenters, long-winded orators might shrink down your speaking slot to a sliver. Pruning your material is the only wise choice. Although your content won't have a chance to impress the audience, your consideration will.

One last observation: If something does go awry, realize that you have the sympathy of the crowd when facing a predicament. So, grab the reins, improvise, and keep the show rolling. Listeners want to have a good experience, too, so a speaker sometimes needs to take charge on behalf of a group.

The saying "Expect the best; prepare for the worst" is attributed to motivational speaker Zig Ziglar. This marriage of naïve optimism and shrewd pragmatism will serve you well as a speaker. In short, don't just prepare a speech; prepare for potential mishaps. In my experience, the more prepared I am, the less that seems to go wrong. When it does, however, we can only aspire to remain as poised as President Bill Clinton. In 1993, with the wrong speech loaded into his teleprompter, Clinton addressed a joint session of Congress and millions of

TV viewers. While his staff scrambled to fix the error, the president extemporized for the first seven minutes of his address. Newspaper headlines around the world praised the speech. More strikingly, former Republican president George H. W. Bush remarked, "The speech he gave was absolutely terrific." Sometimes the backup plan is a blessing in disguise.

14

Exercise Before Speaking

I T'S HARD TO FEEL COURAGEOUS WHEN YOUR HANDS, VOICE, or legs shake. But a surge of adrenaline can leave your muscles twitching like a downed live wire sparking across the blacktop. While practices such as deep breathing and meditation relax some speakers-in-waiting, others can't sit still long enough to generate alpha waves and need to move around to burn off the jitters. For these high-energy folks, a physical problem demands a vigorous physical solution.

Until the parasympathetic nervous system calms down organs revved into overdrive, speakers will sometimes shake from adrenaline overload at the lectern. A simple technique will downshift your racing engine, clear the mind, and restore normal tension levels to the body: Get some exercise before speaking. Any sustained aerobic activity will eventually burn off adrenaline and bring about repose. Walk, jog, swim, bicycle, jump rope, shadowbox, dance, or trot up and down a staircase in the classroom building, office complex, or conference center where you will speak. Well-publicized research, in fact, shows that aerobic exercise simultaneously burns off cortisol, a stress hormone, and prods the pituitary gland into secreting endorphins, the body's natural stress-busting opioids. In plain English, exercise opens the pressure valve and lets your fear-constricted veins and arteries relax.

A few words of advice about using physical exertion to relax: If you don't exercise regularly, don't do anything foolish. Leaping from your favorite armchair to run up and down the stadium bleachers might land you on a stretcher. Stay within your limits. If you do work up a sweat, however, take a warm bath or shower and change into clean clothes before speaking. Good hygiene aids in making a good first impression. Researchers at Loma Linda University also found that immersion in warm water, sometimes called hydrotherapy, relaxes muscles and slightly reduces blood pressure.[5] This will help to soothe your jangled nerves. Finally, don't exercise so vigorously or bathe in water so hot that you feel depleted at the lectern. The goal is to reduce — not drain away — your overstocked energy stores. Save ample energy for the speech.

According to folk wisdom, everything that rises must fall. Regardless, speakers often assume that high anxiety levels will remain constant during a speech. This is untrue. If you present a three-hour-long college lecture or spend six hours teaching in a high school classroom, your body can't maintain peak adrenaline levels for that length of time and you will naturally calm down. The activity of speaking itself also burns away nervous energy. Intense exercise just does this more quickly, rapidly restoring normal arousal levels to the body. So, even if you need to jump rope for ten minutes on the morning of your speech, realize that if you had the chance to talk long enough, your nervous system would eventually curtail anxiety levels and reestablish a comfortable state of homeostasis. Aided by a little common sense, the body's ancient survival systems can serve you as a modern-day speaker.

15

Gain Performance Experience

Howard Gardner just might be a genius. This Harvard professor's insights into human intelligence have radically altered the way we see our gray matter. The slavish dependence on verbal, visual, and quantitative reasoning—pillars of the Stanford-Binet and other IQ tests for decades—has given up ground to Gardner's multidimensional model. In *Frames of Mind*, the psychologist's first attempt to redistrict the intellect, Gardner maps out eight synergistic domains of intelligence: linguistic, spatial, musical, kinesthetic, naturalist, interpersonal, intrapersonal, and logical-mathematical. One of Gardner's most exciting discoveries is that increasing intelligence in one area creates gains in seemingly unrelated sectors. Students who improved their musical abilities at schools testing Gardner's theories, for example, became better at math as well. Given these findings, human intelligence is not locked away in separate, airtight containers, but inhabits one long continuum where mastery of one aptitude improves another.

Professor Gardner, in brief, discovered the intellectual equivalent of cross-training: As swimming laps helps with running, playing music helps with math. The same principle holds true for public address. For years, I've noticed that speakers with a smattering of performance experience typically enjoy stronger public speaking skills. In my case, six months of comedy improvisation bolstered my presentation skills far more than any professional development course I've taken. This lightning-paced, think-on-your-feet, trust-your-gut, remember-there's-an-audience, fly-by-the-seat-of-your-pants, yet-it-all-works-out-in-the-end process is like classroom teaching on an intravenous espresso drip. With no time to think before an improvised response, having days or weeks to prepare a lecture is like child's play. Comedy improv also involves greater risks than teaching, like the time our instructor told the class, "Lay down on the floor! You are strips of bacon frying in a pan! Sizzle and shake! Go for it!" Finally, improvisation employs a broader set of delivery skills than classroom lecturing. At times, I camp it up and indulge in accents, imitations, or overdramatized points to both engage and instruct students.

How can performance experience help with public speaking? In a nutshell, public speaking is the art of skillfully gaining, holding, and releasing an audience's attention. Whenever we put ourselves in front of a crowd, invite their attention, keep it with us, think on our feet, and engage the creative process, we have "spoken" in public, even if the communication is more nonverbal than verbal. Acoustic guitar virtuoso Leo Kottke put it this way: "The principle element in a performance is risk." Whatever the activity, risk-taking leads to growth and confidence, and confidence dissolves fears that inhibit effective performance.

So whether through stage acting, rapping, singing, dance recitals, stand-up comedy, poetry slams, debates, athletic contests, stage bands, marching bands, martial-arts competitions, boxing, performance art, or solo music recitals, spending time in the limelight can add a welcome glow to your public speaking skills. Just find an activity that works for you, have fun while doing it, and bring those feelings of joy and confidence to the lectern when speaking. The activity doesn't matter; cognitive rewiring is the key. The outward process of public speaking will remain the same, but its inward emotional meaning will change. When we perform before others and can say to ourselves, "I'm in front of people, but I'm relaxed. I'm in front of people, but I'm having a good time," we have discovered a magic portal to triumphantly reenter the realm of public address.

16

Get Some More Speech Training

OVER THE YEARS, I'VE TAKEN CLASSES IN COOKING, acting, auto mechanics, ballroom dance, photography, and martial arts. I've also taken private lessons in guitar, voice, and swimming. I'm a lifelong learner, and I'm more than happy to pay an expert to teach me a skill. Why waste months or even years trying to reinvent the wheel? The road ahead may be bumpy and even embarrassing riding around on square wheels.

If you find yourself struggling with the chore of public speaking duties, know that thousands of experts stand at the ready, willing to teach you about the intricacies of public address. Four-year colleges and universities offer comprehensive courses. Community colleges provide affordable, hands-on classes. If you're already enrolled in or have completed a college course, take an advanced class, compete on your school's forensics team, or sign up for a Dale Carnegie seminar. A local chapter of Toastmasters International will also hail you aboard and reacquaint you with the ropes.[6] Many companies also maintain in-house training programs, and adult education is a low-cost alternative in thousands of communities. If pressed for time or living in a rural area, fire up your computer or smartphone for online public speaking instruction. The options are nearly endless.

The rationale for formal speech training is simple: If you don't really know what you're doing and you have to do it in front of others, you're bound to feel nervous. Teachers and trainers to the rescue! Public address has a 2,400-year history, and a well-run speech class offers a simple, time-tested remedy for performance anxiety. First, you will learn how to select, organize, and present ideas—the heart and soul of the speaker's craft; and second, your confidence will soar when you practice and use these skills correctly. Even if you discover that you're already on track during speech instruction, this reassurance will add a few more degrees of swagger to your strut. As added benefits, many classes include tips on combating speech anxiety, and the camaraderie generated among group members facing the same fear—a boot camp on the soapbox, if you will—often cements lasting friendships.

A word of caution for you do-it-yourselfers: Formal speech training offers many advantages over the hit-or-miss results of being self-taught. At a minimum, you can expect a suitable speaking venue, proper equipment, and a sympathetic audience. Ideally, you will also receive feedback from peers, guidance from a seasoned instructor, and a chance to critique yourself on video. This last item alone is worth the price of admission. I know that being filmed sounds scary, but would you arrive at a job interview without checking yourself out in the mirror beforehand? If not, why give a presentation without first knowing what you look and sound like?

A Spanish proverb warns, "Habits are first cobwebs, then cables." With a complex skill such as public speaking, it's easier to correct mistakes early on rather than years later. For some, changing habits can be as painful as breaking and resetting a crooked bone. Despite this commonsense notion, I've coached many professionals who speak as a critical part of their jobs without any special training in the craft. Here's what I've learned from them: Even top-achieving lawyers, doctors, professors, college deans, and chief financial officers feel anxious when they lack sufficient skills or knowledge.

The bottom line? Formal speech training will place you miles ahead of quaking-in-their-boots amateurs and even some high-ranking professionals. So, call now. Operators are standing by. Thousands of colleges, universities, and adult training programs are ready to take your order.

III

Cognitive Strategies

17

Rethink How You Think about Speaking

THE VICTORIAN-ERA COUNTENANCE OF PUBLIC SPEAK-
ing needs a facelift. The term brings to mind ham-fisted
orators with handlebar moustaches harrumphing on bunting-
draped platforms. It also conjures up the prospect of certain
pain—like being strapped into a dentist's chair before the days
of Novocain. Struggling under the weight of these outdated
expectations, many would-be presenters stumble onto the podium and find that what they do naturally—talk—has become
a frightening chore.

The solution to this problem is simple: Change how you
think about public speaking. To dispel its negative overtones,
some academics now call public speaking "presentational
speaking."[1] Why not invent your own user-friendly term for
public address? Call it Public Sharing, Communal Witnessing,
The Big Shout-Out, Show-and-Tell Time, or Everybody-Has-
to-Listen-to-Me Day. Like stepping through the magic mirror in
Alice through the Looking-Glass, a new name can open up a hidden
door to a wondrous new reality.

Do such name changes really matter? It seems so. Search engine BackRub languished in the backwaters of the Internet until 1997, when its founders renamed it Google, one of the most highly valued stocks on the NASDAQ. And who would fare better as a leading man: Thomas Mapother IV or Tom Cruise? Surely the latter. That's why Mr. Mapother adopted his middle name, Cruise, as a surname. Finally, novelist Margaret Mitchell no doubt racked up better sales from *Gone with the Wind* than she would have with *Pansy*, the working title for the book and its main character. As those who hawk products and services know, "The sizzle sells the steak."

This simple marketing strategy has roots in a deeper truth: Language not only describes but shapes our experience of reality. Each term, I witness powerful evidence of this truth. Students with high levels of communication apprehension, such as those suffering from social anxiety disorder, receive permission from counselors to enroll in Interpersonal Communication as a substitute course for Public Speaking. Little do they know about the required presentations in Interpersonal Communication. But we never *call* them presentations—they are "projects." And students' grades are not based on eye contact, vocal delivery, or any other traditional aspect of public address—only content. If a student prefers to sit in a chair and speak, he or she may do so. If a student wants to tote along several pages of original notes, that's okay, too. Much to their delight, by the end of the term a good number of Interpersonal Communication students speak just as confidently and effectively as Public Speaking students.

Should this be a surprise? Not really. We routinely share messages with audiences both large and small without calling it "public speaking." Convince a group of friends to see a film—you've done persuasive speaking; tell your coworkers about the new restaurant around the corner—you've done informative speaking; share kind words with your neighbors about the death of a community member—you've done special occasion speaking, in this case a brief eulogy. Add in social media and electronic communication such as e-mail, Facebook, Twitter, blogging, and whatever else comes next, and we regularly share our perspectives with hundreds if not thousands of people. In short, you don't need a soapbox to practice public communication. Whenever we craft a message for a specific audience, occasion, and purpose, we have engaged in the speaker's craft.

This insight is important for two vital reasons: First, we vastly underestimate the amount of prior experience that we bring to the speaking platform; and second, our emotional experience of public communication is typically a positive one. In fact, our disposition towards communication in general is overwhelmingly favorable. Americans, for example, own and foot the bill for over 320 million cell phones; and those aged eighteen to twenty-four send and receive over 3,200 text messages each month, according to the Pew Center for Internet Research.[2] This is certainly not the behavior of a culture that feels phobic about communication. Because of widespread horror stories, jokes, and surveys that villainize public address, however, we mindlessly throw it under the bus without realizing how often we take a similar journey and enjoy the sights and sounds.

Pablo Picasso once observed, "Every child is an artist. The problem is how to remain an artist once he grows up." Similarly, we're all born public speakers, and the challenge is to remain outspoken as adults. Fears needlessly arise when we see "public speaking" as an activity totally divorced from our day-to-day communications. If you *think* of public speaking in a new way—as a natural extension of your daily discourse—you will *experience* it in a new way. So, keep on sharing with the rest of the community. Give a "speech" from time to time when the need arises, but we all know that you're just shouting to your friends on the neighborhood playground.

18

Focus on the Benefits of Presenting

THE HUMAN MIND OFTEN FOCUSES ON THE NEGATIVE. The daily news doesn't help much either. Each morning and evening there is a blizzard of bad news: fires, murders, lay-offs, car wrecks, hurricanes, foreclosures, and political scandals. Add in a nightly dose of crime dramas and, by adulthood, we are seasoned detectives who instinctively ferret out the negative. It's no wonder that students enrolled in a public speaking course turn this doom-seeking radar on themselves. The question often haunting a novice speaker's mind is not "How well will I do?" but "What *will* go wrong when I speak?"

I have some fun with this pessimism in speech class. I pass out index cards and ask students to write down their fears. They divide these fears into three categories — physical, mental, and social. That is, what might go awry with the body, mind, or audience reactions during a speech? The end result is a gut-wrenching avalanche of speaking horrors. Sometimes, I joke around and dramatize the worst-case scenario after the exercise: "So, you're afraid that you'll turn red, shake like a leaf, lose control of all your bodily functions, pass out, stammer, forget your name, forget everything you've prepared, spew out cuss words like a sailor, and then go blank and stare at the back wall. Meanwhile, the audience judges you as boring, stupid, and a total failure. Is that all that's bothering you?"

After a few chuckles of relief, we get down to the serious business of changing the class's mindset. Asking ourselves what will go wrong when we speak is a self-defeating question. So, I change the question and challenge the class by asking, "What will go *right* when you speak? How might giving a presentation benefit both you and the audience?"

From this new perspective the class brainstorms a much different set of outcomes. I list them on the whiteboard:

I will learn about public speaking, a workplace skill in great demand.

I will stand up to one of the greatest fears that human beings face.

My audience will learn something valuable from me that they can apply to their lives.

I will experience power and self-confidence that I didn't know I had.

I will see myself in a new and more positive light.

I will share interesting parts of myself, and others will come to know and like me.

I will discover a hidden talent for speaking.

I will grow as a person.

The mood in the room lightens. My marker goes down. Hallelujah! Let the good times roll.

Back in your armchair at home, didn't it feel much better reading this second list than the first? If so, create your own calming list by using this simple remedy for speech anxiety. Before any speaking engagement, focus on all the good that might come from it. If you like categories, get out a piece of paper and brainstorm social, mental, vocational, financial, material, physical, spiritual, recreational, and personal growth benefits that can flow into your life through public speaking. When a fear comes to mind, gently remind yourself of the many positive outcomes that public address can bestow on your life.

Mark Twain wrote, "I am an old man and have known a great many troubles, but most of them never happened." In reality, the outcomes we fear rarely, if ever, happen. Most often the good happens. Keep this in mind at the lectern.

19

Fear Management, Not Extinction, Is the Goal

I F YOU PICKED UP THIS BOOK HOPING TO TOTALLY ELIMINATE the fear of public speaking, you will be disappointed. *Speak with Courage* was a carefully chosen book title. Although a provocative moniker such as *Fearless Speaking* might sell more copies, it's just not honest. Consider this example: After performing thousands of live concerts over a twenty-three-year period, tallying up more than 150 gold singles and albums, racking up record sales of over one billion units, garnering fourteen Grammy nominations, and starring in thirty-three feature films, Elvis Presley said, "I've never gotten over what they call stage fright. I go through it every show." Even the King of Rock 'n' Roll got the shakes.

Why is this? Put briefly, human experience does not change human nature. During a typical day, dozens if not hundreds of wants and needs drive us. We want to jump out of bed when the alarm clock rings, eat breakfast, arrive at work or school on time, make a positive impression on our boss or teacher, be liked and accepted by others, make it home by dinnertime, savor an enjoyable meal, hit the gym, spend time with those we care about, do some reading, watch a favorite show on television, call a friend, go to bed at a reasonable hour, and enjoy a good night's sleep. In the morning, we wake up and do it all over again. When a threat stands in the way of attaining these small daily goals or our life's larger purposes, we feel anxious. It's that simple. We feel fear in response to threat or danger, and there is always a danger that we will not get what we want or need in this world.

To frame things poetically, fear is the shadow of desire. If you want a promotion at work, you create the fear of getting passed over. If you want an A in class, you create the fear of getting a B. If you want someone to return your romantic interest, you create the fear of rejection. When desire is born, the fear of being denied is also born. Desire and fear emerge simultaneously from the womb of the human psyche as Siamese twins, and like twins of a bygone era hopelessly joined at the hip, they will spend a lifetime together.

I see this dynamic play out in speech class each term. Sometimes the straight-A students are the most anxious. They worry about GPAs, scholarships, attaining degrees, acceptance into competitive graduate programs, and starting their careers. The prospect of a B or C in speech class is nearly intolerable for them. At the other end of the report-card spectrum, the likeable slackers can be more relaxed as speakers, albeit sharing second-rate material at times.

That leads to our next point. Although popular wisdom would have us aim above the target to avoid falling short, a better strategy is counterintuitive: Have realistic expectations. If you expect to feel supremely confident during a talk while folks roll in the aisles over your jokes, you may be in for a surprise. To paraphrase John Lennon of the Beatles, the actual speech may be what happens to you while you're busy making other plans. In fact, communication research establishes that speakers with modest expectations fare better than presenters with lofty ambitions. And this makes sense, particularly for beginning speakers. While goal setting is a valuable practice, the weight of unrealistically high expectations will only compound routine fears about public speaking. If you're worried about remembering your opening lines, for example, trying to memorize the entire speech to impress an audience is an unnecessary burden. Why put all that added pressure on yourself? If you give a stellar speech, great; if not, you can still do a good job.

Here's an insider secret: Make peace with the fact that fear will never end until you reach nirvana and settle for the goal of skillfully *managing* fear. Imagine a scale from zero to ten, where zero represents no fear and ten represents sheer jugular-popping terror. In the eight-to-ten range, you will probably be too nervous to tie your own shoes, let alone give a presentation. But from zero to three you may lack the drive and energy to really put yourself out there and connect with an audience. Between four and seven your pulse may have quickened, but the pounding in your ears will not deafen you. Your goal is to keep fear within this manageable range by using your wits, experience, and the strategies in this book.

Some years ago No Fear apparel was very popular. Although a catchy marketing slogan, it's a poor fit for reality. When our EKG and EEG flatline, the pulse of fear will also flatline. In the meantime, whether facing the acute challenge of public speaking or other garden-variety risks, we can do no better than heed the advice of South Africa's first black president, Nelson Mandela. In his autobiography, *Long Walk to Freedom*, the Nobel Peace Prize winner wrote, "I learned that courage was not the absence of fear, but the triumph over it."

Take that wisdom to the lectern with you.

20

Take Baby Steps

I N *THE WAY OF LIFE*, CHINESE SAGE LAO TZU WROTE, "THE journey of a thousand miles begins with a single step." Applied to public speaking, this 2,600-year-old wisdom means giving ourselves the compassion and permission to take things at a reasonable pace. The race does not always go to the swift, as Aesop's fable "The Tortoise and the Hare" reminds us.

College students sometimes adopt this gradual approach to public address without realizing it. A fair number register for public speaking three or four times before completing the course. To begin the process, they register and drop *before* the first class. Then they register and drop *after* the first class. The next time they register and hang around through the first speech. Finally, they soldier on through the entire term. This hide-and-seek process is expensive and time-consuming, so consciously working through a series of manageable steps the first time around seems like a wiser approach.

At times, psychology takes folk wisdom and turns it into science. The homespun advice of taking baby steps translates into systematic desensitization, a method to safely and gradually reduce the anxiety associated with our most daunting fears. The process involves just a few simple steps: Imagine what you fear most through least about public speaking, draw up a graduated list of these communication scenarios, and then imagine each scary vignette while in a relaxed state. With this easy-to-climb staircase before you, you now have a pathway to personal growth and success beckoning at your feet.

To prime the pump for your own brainstorming session, I've drawn up a sample list of ten possible speaking fears. Since we're all wired differently, no two rankings will ever be the same. This hierarchy is just an example: Thinking about giving a speech, researching a speech, outlining a speech, giving the presentation in your mind's eye, rehearsing in a room by yourself, recording and watching yourself on video, practicing in front of a friend, rehearsing in front of a small group, practicing in the room where you will actually speak, and, finally, giving the speech.

After creating your own hierarchy of fears, diligently work through each in succession. If using systematic desensitization by the book, you will *imagine* each scenario before trying out any risky behavior. Visualizing scary scenes before hazarding flesh-and-blood encounters offers a safe way to both meet fears and practice success. If feeling bolder, simply test out the behaviors one by one in real time. Whichever route you take, don't rush. Your goal is to feel at ease with each scenario *before* moving on to the next. Think of it like the Panama Canal — until a ship rises to the water level of the next lock, it can't move forward. Similarly, your progress during systematic desensitization should be driven internally by your own comfort level, not externally by the clock or calendar.

Psychologists rely on another strategy that lies outside the realm of folk wisdom when using systematic desensitization: deep relaxation. In clinical terms, pairing a relaxed state with a scary stimulus counterconditions or retrains the body and mind to respond in a calmer manner. For example, while engaged in yoga, a walk in the park, or listening to soft music, imagine yourself giving a speech. These enjoyable activities will give your fears a rosier hue.

All this looks great on the chalkboard, but what takes a few minutes to sketch out by hand can take a few months — or years — to work through in real life. Be patient with yourself. If a step feels too hot underfoot when you hike up to that vantage point, circle back and create an intervening step. For example, if leaping from rehearsing alone to practicing in front of a group feels too scary, make an audio recording of your speech and ask a supportive friend to listen. Taking two steps forward and one step back will still move you forward.

Whether using systematic desensitization, some variation of it, or your own method, there is organic wisdom in a gradual approach. Each flower opens in its own season. Or, in workaday terms, effective speakers often stand on planks of self-confidence that are hewn and laid in place over the course of many years. From time to time, I hear from former students who now work as teachers or public servants, or who take center stage in the media or performing arts. One former student — brawny yet painfully shy when he was eighteen years old — now works as a radio show host and TV sports commentator after an eleven-year career as a professional athlete. He is also a motivational speaker. Like many of my students, when first stepping into a public speaking classroom, he would have never imagined himself addressing audiences of thousands or millions.

Rome wasn't built in a day. Progress, not perfection. Slow and steady wins the race. There are dozens of clichéd ways of expressing this chapter's already clichéd title, but its authentic promise remains clear: Having the patience and persistence to take a series of unremarkable steps can lead to a remarkable outcome. Once upon a future time, you might be the tortoise that crosses the finish line ahead of the hare, and that is the storied moral of this fable.

21

It's All in Your Head

WATCHING THOUSANDS OF STUDENTS GIVE SPEECHES IS interesting. The classroom situation is the same, but their reactions are strikingly different. It's the same setting with the same lectern and the same teacher, but students' wants, needs, beliefs, histories, attitudes, and expectations shape markedly different experiences. Some have a great time; others suffer needlessly.

Many students can easily point to the source of their anxiety—the audience. On an assigned speech day, the early birds often volunteer to speak first if fewer students are present at the beginning of class. Each new audience member compounds anxiety for these fledgling speakers. Like the proverbial straw that broke the camel's back, some imaginary number of audience members might create an emotional burden so great that a speaker would collapse under its psychic weight. To the beginner's mind, the audience is a necessary evil—or just plain evil. If speeches could be given without them, it would be a perfect world.

Since we can't eliminate the "public" from "public speaking," how do we exorcise the inner demon of fear? Do we need a cross, garlic, holy water, and a wooden stake to drive out the beast? Hardly. Let's start with a simple tool. Go to a room with a mirror and peer into the looking glass. What do you see? Yourself? Are you afraid? You should be. You stand face to face with the person who creates all of your fears. Radio, television, or passing alien spaceships don't pipe them into your head. They bubble up from within.

A brief story will illustrate the power of our perceptions. One morning my friend Will sat in the Los Angeles train station mindlessly staring off into space. A husky male voice challenged him from across the aisle: "What are you looking at?"

"Nothing," Will said.

The man confronted him again more angrily, "What are you looking at?"

"Nothing," Will said, "I'm blind."

No longer feeling defensive, the stranger softened his stance and apologized. In truth, nothing about the situation had changed except the way the man saw it. Will has suffered from retinitis pigmentosa since childhood and gradually lost his vision, but the sighted man's perceptions temporarily blinded him to the reality of his own circumstances.

In the mid-1950s, psychologist Albert Ellis developed Rational Emotive Behavior Therapy. This school of psycho-therapy rests on a simple assumption: Beliefs generate feelings. In the above example, the offending thoughts might sound like this: "That man is staring at me. People should not stare at each other. He is making me angry." What the stranger told himself generated feelings of anger and defensiveness, not my friend's behavior. To map this out visually, it's *not* A (event) → C (emotion); rather, it's A (event) → B (belief) → C (emotion). Everything we perceive gets filtered through the mind before emotions percolate into being. Because we each see the same events differently, the same events can trigger wildly different feelings for each of us. The winning side feels ecstatic after victory; the losing side slinks away. We, not events, create our feelings.

A vital corollary follows in Ellis's theory: To change our feelings, we must change our beliefs. With this axiom in mind, you can work on the root cause of speech anxiety—your own misguided thoughts. What scary things do you tell yourself about public speaking? About audiences? About how you should perform? What limiting beliefs do you have about your own talents, worth, or intelligence?

Let's find out. Get out a piece of paper and draw a line down the middle. On one side, write down every negative belief or expectation that you have about public speaking in general and about yourself as a speaker. On the other side, balance each fear with a more supportive thought. For example, the left side of the page might say, "Everyone will hate my speech!" while the right half could say, "Many people will like what I have to say." The left side might read, "Everyone will know I'm scared to death," while the right side counters with, "I may feel nervous, but I'll put that energy to good use." Do this for every negative belief. If a new fear crops up, jot it down and create another antidote. From time to time before speaking, review your notes and reinforce these positive, supportive thoughts.

Over the ages, human beings have clung to many erroneous beliefs. We once thought that the sun revolved around a flat earth, that diseases sprung from imbalances among four bodily fluids called *humors*, and that women were inferior to and the property of men. In similar fashion, voices from a bygone era may have misled you about the true nature of public speaking. Be open to the possibility that it's a creature of an entirely different order. It is not evil. It can be fun. It can be exhilarating. It can be deeply fulfilling. Just believe it, and you will see it.

22

Break the Boulder into Stepping-Stones

I GREW UP IN A TOWN ALONG A RIVER NOT FAR FROM A ROCK quarry. While he drove us past the quarry on a family trip, I asked my father, a police officer, what took place behind its iron gates. He explained that shackled prisoners broke large rocks into gravel with heavy sledgehammers. Like an inmate sentenced to hard labor, unless we take the time to break down the boulder of fear into stepping-stones, we may never feel free as public speakers and our ideas will remain needlessly imprisoned.

Novice presenters sometimes become paralyzed by this boulder of fear standing in their path. Its icy shadow freezes all rational thought, and they see no way through it, around it, under it, or over it. The seconds slowly and thunderously tick by until the dreaded moment to speak arrives. Little preparation occurs before the appointed hour because the task at hand seems so overwhelming. Although one liberating blast of dynamite that shatters the boulder standing in our way would be a godsend, chipping away at the offending stone a bit at a time is a more realistic escape plan. But how do we do that?

Everyone knows that people fear giving speeches, but what—specifically—do *you* fear? You will never conquer a nameless and faceless enemy, but given shape and form, you can calculate weaknesses and plot an attack. To aid in this effort, many public speaking textbooks define common elements of the speaking situation: topic, audience, occasion, setting, and speaker.

Before the date of your presentation, review each element and ask yourself what fears, if any, come to mind. Start with the first and work your way through the list. Does something unsettle you about the material you've chosen for the topic? Adjust the content. Are you uncertain how someone or some portion of the audience will respond? Do further audience analysis and put yourself at ease. Are you unsure if your speaking style or comments are appropriate for the occasion? Check in with a trusted mentor for guidance. Do you feel uncomfortable with the setting? Review "Familiarize Yourself with the Speech Setting" (Chapter 12), and scope out the speaking venue. Do you doubt your own level of preparedness? Research and rehearse until you feel more confident.

This simple step-by-step process forces you to dig into your personal geology and discover each distinct stratum that runs through *your* boulder of fear. By creating a specific plan for each fear, you will break down the towering monolith blocking your path into a series of manageable stepping-stones. If you fear five things, each plan can reduce your fear by 20 percent. Five fears and five plans make possible a 100 percent reduction. This basic arithmetic will free your feet from the muck of anxiety and get you moving again.

Nothing captures the spirit of this rational inquiry better than scientist Marie Curie's observation: "Nothing in life is to be feared. It is only to be understood." Fear thrives in the darkness of ignorance. By bringing specific fears to light and creating an antidote for each, you will feel an uplifting sense of control and mastery. Unlike some of the unfortunate prisoners in the rock quarry, a judge didn't hand you a life sentence. On closer inspection, the boulder that once stood in your way will reveal within itself a pathway to success lined with well-placed stepping-stones.

23

Fill in the Blanks with
Sentence-Completion Exercises

Feeling uneasy about his upcoming voyage, Stephen Jenkin turned back for home, emptied his pockets, and left his watch, jewelry, and personal effects with his parents. According to author George Behe, Jenkin did this "in case he never returned." His fear was well founded. On April 10, 1912, Jenkin boarded the "unsinkable" *Titanic* in Southampton, England, and rode her to the bottom of the sea.[3]

As this story suggests, fears that seem unreasonable on the surface — like not wanting to sail on an "unsinkable" ship — can hold great value for us. Had Mr. Jenkin fully heeded his misgivings, he might have sidestepped a fatal voyage. Similarly, speakers sometimes feel afraid without consciously knowing or acknowledging what they fear. Vague hints and clues taunt us but don't quite take shape. Only by identifying specific fears, however, can we concoct remedies to treat those fears. Which potion will work best: eye of newt or wing of bat? Where is that all-knowing crystal ball?

Our do-it-yourself culture offers a roll-up-your-shirtsleeves option for peering into ourselves. Filling in your mental blanks with sentence-completion exercises is an effective alternative to hypnosis and the psychiatrist's leather couch. Used as an English grammar exercise by generations of students, psychologist Nathaniel Branden utilized sentence-completion exercises to work through emotional issues with clients rather than fragmented sentences. While some techniques in this book, such as "Break the Boulder into Stepping-Stones" (Chapter 22), capitalize on rational, linear thinking, this strategy caters to creative, nonlinear thinking. Since true insights reveal novel perspectives, we can't always move from ignorance to insight by walking lockstep along a well-known path.

The tools you will need to try sentence-completion exercises are cheap and easy to find: a pen, a pad of paper, and an open mind. The process is also simple. Jot down a sentence stem at the top of a blank piece of paper and then fill in as many responses as you can. If you like, burn candles or incense, or play soothing music to set the mood. Helpful insights arise from completing each sentence stem with whatever first comes to mind, no matter how silly, offbeat, or surprising. In Freudian terms, give your superego the night off. Don't bite your tongue. Grant yourself permission to say anything. What you scribble on paper can't harm you or others.

This exercise addresses two common speaking problems: unearthing what you truly fear and creating strategies to calm those fears. Composing original sentence stems works best, but here are some samples to get you started on the task of identifying fears:

When I speak, I am afraid that . . .
If I was really honest with myself, I would admit that I fear . . .
Something I believe about public speaking that gets in my way is . . .

When responding to these and other sentence stems, write as much as you like, filling page after page if needed. The results may surprise you. The sentence stem "When I speak, I am afraid that," for example, may be followed by "I will sound like SpongeBob SquarePants" or "People will smell my sweat." Honor these nuggets of honesty.

Besides taking you off guard, your responses may cluster into groups. If so, circle recurring themes. Fears about forgetting or looking nervous may reappear in different guises. You're onto something when this happens. Psssst! Wanna know another secret? During a similar exercise in my speech classes, students anonymously write down their fears on index cards. When we pull the cards out of a hat and read them aloud, students discover that they all fear the same things. Likewise, if you could peer over a friend's shoulder as he or she worked on a sentence-completion exercise, you might think you were stealing a glance at your own journal.

After identifying your fears, use the same process on another page to explore possible solutions. A few sentence stems for this task follow:

> *I feel most comfortable speaking when . . .*
> *I could really help myself as a speaker by . . .*
> *What would really help me to get over the fear of public speaking is . . .*

Again, don't edit your responses. What seems like an offbeat idea at first glance may turn out to be a great help. Like the first part of the exercise, your answers may fall into patterns. Circle any recurring themes to identify on-target strategies for allaying fears. By implementing these ideas, heretofore hidden and unknown, you will feel more at ease while speaking since you have already grappled with the demons that *truly* haunt you.

The *Titanic* sank on April 15, 1912, after swerving to avoid a visible iceberg. What doomed the largest passenger ship afloat was the concealed base of the iceberg lurking just below the waterline. Similarly, fears lingering beneath the threshold of consciousness can sabotage your best speaking efforts. If you've done research and rehearsed but don't realize that a morbid fear of forgetting is your Achilles' heel, you might still freeze up at the lectern. While the *Titanic* will forever remain in her watery grave, sentence-completion exercises gently bring submerged fears into the light where they finally have a chance to melt away.

24

Demolish Fear with Implosion Therapy

IN THE DEAD OF WINTER, DARING MEMBERS OF POLAR BEAR clubs plunge into frigid lakes and oceans wearing just summer bathing suits. Some hack holes through ice-encrusted waters to honor the breathtaking tradition. This practice captures the spirit of implosion therapy: It's a headfirst dive into the abyss, not a dip-your-toe-in-the-pool-and-get-used-to-the-cold-an-inch-at-a-time approach to fear. After all, slowly doing something painful—whether removing a tooth or a Band-Aid—doesn't make it any less painful.

Pioneered by psychologist Thomas Stampfl in the 1960s, implosion therapy, sometimes called "flooding," postulates that massive amounts of exposure to feared stimuli reduces or elimi-nates the anxiety associated with them. In layman's terms, if turtles terrify you, camping out overnight in a glade crawling with terrapins should take the edge off. When the mind sees there is nothing to fear, the alarm bells grow silent, and we relax into a new and less threatening reality.

Within the first fifteen minutes of the first day of public speaking class, I have all the students in front of the room belting out a well-known quotation together. By the end of that initial meeting, students will have been on their feet to talk three times. The suspense of when they will speak and what it will feel like is over, and—lo and behold—they live to tell the tale.

How can you apply this strategy to your own presentations? While it's impractical to lock yourself in a room and give speeches to a hostile egg-and-tomato-throwing crowd for hours on end, there are other creative options. First, rehearse in front of a live audience of supportive friends over and over again, well before your scheduled presentation date. To avoid rote memorization of a speech, talk about other topics or give impromptu speeches. If the thought of an unruly mob terrifies you, have your practice audience heckle you—all in good fun, of course—to move past that fear. Next, do a lot of speaking. Speak at work, school, and the corner bus stop if they let you. Join a chapter of Toastmasters International. Take a Dale Carnegie seminar. The more you speak, the less anxious you will feel. Finally, if short on practice time, vividly replay your most-feared speaking scenario in your mind's eye. There you are—naked, drooling, beet-red, and throwing up on the lectern—over and over again, in slow motion if you prefer. Like writing "I will not pass notes in class" one hundred times on the blackboard, the emotional charge of these taboo imaginings will soon lose their potency and fade away.

A word of caution about implosion therapy: Please distinguish between healthy and neurotic fears. Fear of going over Niagara Falls in a barrel is a healthy fear. Since the first attempt by Annie Taylor in 1901, daredevils have suffocated in barrels, sunk to the bottom lashed to anvils, and been smashed to smithereens on the unforgiving rocks at the base of the falls. On the other hand, the fears of dirt, mice, elevators, thunderstorms, or public speaking are all unwarranted. These phobias hold us back and limit our lives when they shouldn't. Use implosion therapy to root out neurotic fears rather than legitimate anxieties.

Eleanor Roosevelt, a political force in her own right and First Lady to Franklin Delano Roosevelt, said, "I believe that anyone can conquer fear by doing the things he fears to do." Psychologist Albert Ellis took this advice to heart. Very shy about dating as a young man, in just one month he approached 130 different women who sat alone on park benches near his office. Thirty walked away immediately, but one hundred stayed and spoke with him; one agreed to a date. The risk paid off. Dr. Ellis overcame his fear of dating, got married, and went on to write over a dozen books on relationships. With self-administered implosion therapy, experiencing *more* rather than *less* of what you fear may be just what the speech doctor ordered.

25

Try Gestalt Chairwork

I N THE SUMMER OF 1858, ECHOING A PASSAGE FROM THE New Testament, then Illinois U.S. Senate nominee Abraham Lincoln remarked that a "house divided against itself cannot stand." When part of us wants to speak and another part holds us back, when part of us is free and another part shackled by fear, we approach the lectern with a civil war raging inside.

Gestalt psychology offers a unique way to resolve conflict when we are of two minds. This humanistic school of therapy seeks to uncover, express, and reconcile conflicted parts of ourselves that drain energy, get acted out unknowingly, and stand in the way of peace of mind and wholeness — noble goals indeed. Since speech is a key milestone in childhood development, public speaking can trigger dormant fears from the distant past. Gestalt invites dialogue with disowned parts of ourselves — maybe even that scared little kid inside — so that we can walk up to the lectern feeling whole.

The empty-chair technique, otherwise known as "chairwork," is a mainstay of Gestalt practice. To begin this form of role-playing, place two empty chairs across from each other. Next, bring an unresolved conflict to mind. While sitting in one chair, vividly imagine the part of yourself you are in conflict with sitting in the opposite chair. For example, one part can be the side of you that wants to speak, while in the other chair sits the scared you that doesn't want to speak. Now comes the fun part: Begin a dialogue with the unoccupied chair. When one side has spoken its piece, switch chairs and speak from the opposing point of view. Continue this dialogue until you express the needs and interests of both parties, staking out common ground and a path to resolution.

Following a few simple ground rules will help you to get the most from the empty-chair technique. First, don't edit. No matter how silly or unexpected your responses seem, let them bubble up and out. Assume that every remark holds something of value for you. Second, don't interrupt; don't cut yourself off. Let pieces of you that ordinarily whisper in hushed tones trumpet their needs and feelings. Third, embrace the process with the innocence of a three-year-old talking to an imaginary friend at a make-believe tea party. For the moment, let unicorns roam the earth. Fourth, your goal is to negotiate a peace settlement, so strive for an agreement while exploring the conflict. Only do so, however, after both sides have spoken their piece and feel at ease. Fifth, don't rush. As you move from chair to chair, settle into character before speaking, and then fully express your views and sentiments before switching sides. Finally, since you don't know what will come up during the empty-chair process, lock the door, draw the shades, and hold the dialogue alone or in the company of a supportive friend or counselor. Feeling self-conscious will only skew the results.

Here's what an empty chair dialogue might sound like:

"So, tell me why you don't want to give that talk next Monday."

"I'm scared to death. I might pee my pants. And what if I throw up? Have you even thought about that? I don't think so, Ms. Hotshot!"

"Honestly, I didn't know you felt that scared. But now I see how worried you are."

"Heck yeah! And what if I pass out? What are you going to do then? That would look real cool, right? Fainting in front of that tyrant of a boss!"

"So, you're afraid of peeing your pants and then throwing up and fainting, especially in front of the boss?"

"Yeah! I don't look good covered in vomit. It will clash with my shoes."

"And that would be embarrassing, too. Let me ask you then, is there anything we can do to make this scary stuff seem less scary?"

"Hmmm, let me think. Well, don't eat a bean-and-cheese burrito with jalapeño peppers before speaking. That makes my stomach feel queasy."

"OK. That's a good idea. What else comes to mind?"

"Don't drink a ton of coffee either. And go to the bathroom before you speak."

"Anything else?"

"You know what? A reward would be nice, too. How about a movie afterwards to relax? Sometimes I work really hard and you don't even seem to notice."

"OK. I'm willing to do that. And I'm sorry if it seems like I don't notice. I do."

The above example, artificially brief, nonetheless captures the heart of the process. From empty chairs spring hidden thoughts, wants, and feelings. When I first tried this technique during peer-counselor training, I admit it seemed goofy and way out there. Hey, I'm from the East Coast. Talk to myself? Didn't

Mom tell me not to do that? But it worked, and I felt better afterwards. So why not give it a shot? If done in good faith, rusted doors lurch open, the unknown becomes known, and conflicted parts of you become allies.

At the start of every boxing match the referee instructs both pugilists to "shake hands and come out fighting." With successful chairwork, aspects of yourself previously in conflict will shake hands and come out fighting. Now undivided, they can align themselves against a common foe—speech anxiety.

26

Shyness Is Not a Crime

WHEN MY BROTHER WAS FIVE YEARS OLD, HE BROUGHT home a girl from the neighborhood, put on a record in the living room, and said, "Let's dance!" My stunned parents sat watching in their armchairs, witnessing boldness in their son they could never match. The world was made for people like my brother. Job ads look for aggressive, outgoing sales types able to multitask in a fast-paced environment. The Nike slogan "Just Do It" sums up the zeitgeist of modern life. Caught up in a swirl of texting, facebooking, and tweeting, the world seems bent on action and interaction rather than reflection and solitude.

When it comes to belly buttons, most people are innies rather than outies. The opposite holds true for personalities: Most people are extraverts rather than introverts.[4] The user's manual for the Myers-Briggs Type Indicator® (MBTI), the oldest and most commonly used personality test, once estimated that 75 percent of Americans are extraverted. I often recognize extraverts on the first day of class. They're the ones with 783 friends on Facebook and thumbs that move at warp speed to intercept the incoming meteor shower of text messages. The shy students in class sometimes feel envious of these naturally outgoing peers. After all, if being the center of attention is your idea of cruel and unusual punishment, a semester-length public speaking course is like stepping into the iron maiden.

Carl Jung, whose theories undergird the MBTI, was the first psychologist to identify extraversion and introversion as innate, lifelong preferences. Extraverts like to turn outwards, drawing energy from the world of people and activity, while introverts choose solitude and quiet time for renewal. This doesn't mean that extraverts care more about others or have superior social skills; they just like to chew the fat more often with the herd. Henry David Thoreau, on the other hand, captured the widely contrasting sentiments of the introvert: "I never found the companion that was so companionable as solitude."

Introverts sometimes enter my public speaking class feeling stigmatized, and rightly so. If likened to books, they have often been judged by a glance at the cover. What is normal to them has at best been misconstrued as meek, polite, or withdrawn behavior and at worst as backwards, unfriendly, or antisocial conduct. To the uninitiated, introverted speakers can seem cool, aloof, and distant. Nothing could be further from the truth. Nestled within a rich and complex inner world, introverts—like Beethoven, Bill Gates, and Emily Dickinson—often experience deep thoughts, intense feelings, and profound loyalties. As the old saying goes, "Still waters run deep." The surface may appear calm, but the depths churn with life-giving currents.

Extraverts, feel free to hit the showers now or just sit quietly on the bench and listen: It's time for the locker-room pep talk. Introverts, take heart! Although a true minority without any protective legislation, you wield several natural advantages in the realm of public speaking. First, you were born to be trailblazers in the inner world. The lofty sphere of theories, ideas, and imaginings is your native domain, and a good speaker often acts as a tour guide in this rich wilderness. Second, over many years and many thousands of speeches, I've noticed that the talks of introverts can be clearer and more organized than those of their chummier classmates. Your ducks are more apt to waddle in a row. Perhaps energy that gets shunted outwards among the more gregarious gets shunted inwards among the introverted, fueling greater proficiencies in the cognitive domain. As a case in point, a study of gifted children by the Child Development Center of Colorado found that over 75 percent of children with IQs soaring above 160 were introverts.[5]

Along with the advantages of introversion, however, come some disadvantages. Many introverts display only modest degrees of vocal and physical animation. As a result, they can be less engaging than their grinning, slap-you-on-the-back counterparts. To warm up this misleading air of detachment, modest speakers must externalize their interior engagement. That is, they should increase eye contact along with vocal and physical expressiveness to both engage and connect with an audience.

This new public posture might require a bit of stretching for some. Susan Cain, for example, an introvert and author of the seminal book *Quiet: The Power of Introverts in a World That Can't Stop Talking*, confided that she needed a full year of coaching before delivering a twenty-minute TED talk. Here's my advice for inching that quivering big toe into the spotlight. During practice sessions, force yourself to use several gestures during each sentence. Although it may feel unnatural at first, over time you will develop fluid and natural movements. While beneficial for many presenters, increasing volume and vocal variety can be particularly helpful for reserved speakers. Record your speeches to see and hear yourself as others do. What may seem as over-the-top as a used-car commercial during a practice session may sound just right on playback. Unassuming speakers don't particularly like this look-at-me behavior, but during a speech the audience is looking at you anyway. Just look back and grin. Like it or not, public speaking contains elements of showmanship. An engaging stage presence, even if part of an alter ego, can boost your speaking IQ.

In closing, keep in mind that introverts stand in good company, historically. Evidence suggests that Sir Isaac Newton, Abraham Lincoln, Marie Curie, Albert Einstein, and Mother Teresa were of the quieter persuasion, but they fared well in life. So if you step onto the podium as an introvert, marching to the beat of a different drummer, know that you do so in the esteemed company of these and other kindred spirits.

27

Try the Talking Cure

Bᴇʀᴛʜᴀ Pᴀᴘᴘᴇɴʜᴇɪᴍ ɪs ɴᴏᴛ ᴀ ʜᴏᴜsᴇʜᴏʟᴅ ɴᴀᴍᴇ, ʙᴜᴛ her catchphrase is well known. In the late 1800s, this troubled young woman entered psychoanalysis with Dr. Josef Breuer, a colleague of Sigmund Freud. Breuer tried technique after technique with his patient, but nothing seemed to work. In his opinion, he had failed as a psychiatrist. Ms. Pappenheim nevertheless professed to a marked improvement. In fact, the more deeply he listened, the better she felt. Protected then by the pseudonym "Anna O.," Bertha Pappenheim underwent what she called "the talking cure." Her experience confirmed that listening itself, apart from any therapeutic technique, has the power to heal and ground.

I frequently see evidence of this on speech day. When I enter the classroom, the air buzzes with chatter about the dreaded task at hand. Half the room listens (not scheduled to speak) and the other half talks (scheduled to speak). This release of pent-up tension is healthy and normal. Talking about our troubles can reduce the weight of a burden, normalize our experiences, dissipate the strength of anxieties, and bring possible solutions into focus. Fears grow in the dark and wither in the light. Ask any child: Imaginary monsters disappear with the flick of a switch.

Fortunately, many of us enjoy a wide variety of options for having a heart-to-heart talk. Most folks feel empathy for those giving presentations, so friends, relatives, classmates, and coworkers might lend a sympathetic ear. Often, these familiar ears are enough to still our troubled waters. Support groups and twelve-step programs also welcome our unburdening. For those who prefer individual counseling, traditional psychotherapy and peer or cocounseling offer private consolation. If you are living on a budget, college campuses or community mental health centers offer low or no-cost counseling. Anxiety and insecurity that arise from abusive or traumatic experiences, however, have deeper roots. Consult with a professional who can skillfully untangle these confining cords.

If you're the go-it-alone type, all this "let's talk it out" hooey might seem like a bunch of nonsense, but public address is a complex experience that stirs strong emotions for many. Our bodies, voices, ideas, and manner of speaking are all subjected to public scrutiny. Some presentations involve self-disclosure, which adds another layer of risk. Other topics require controversial stances on sensitive issues. In addition, the acute fear of public speaking often amplifies day-to-day anxieties, so chinks in our armor spread farther apart, leaving some speakers feeling quite vulnerable. When their mental engines sputter and stall at the lectern, even the most rebellious students will look at me with an urgent need for approval. This is no surprise. Our first teachers taught us how to say "mama" and "dada," so the hunger for reassurance while trying out new syllables in public stretches far back into infancy.

While on the topic of support, let me offer a few words of encouragement for the gentlemen reading this chapter. Despite changing times, popular culture still portrays men *acting out* rather than *talking out* strong emotions. Sadly, this stereotype is reflected by some tragic statistics. In her book *How Not to Die*, medical examiner Dr. Jan Garavaglia points out that men are twice as likely to die in car accidents, three times as likely to drown, four times as likely to commit suicide, and eight times more likely to be murder victims than women. Studies also show that men develop less intimate friendships and are more reluctant to enter counseling than women. Not surprisingly, women around the world outlive men.

Gentlemen, take heart. Our testosterone needn't be a free pass to oblivion. As many men already know, confiding in another—whether a friend or counselor—is just another tool in life's toolkit. You won't get kicked out of any worthwhile fraternity if you talk about your fears. It takes courage to open up and reveal vulnerabilities; it takes no guts to clam up.

Whether male or female, respect your inborn need to share life's ups and downs. Giving a speech is one of the scariest things that many people will ever do. Facing this unnerving task without seeking support just doesn't make a lot of sense. Would you try bungee jumping or mountain climbing, for example, without talking with a friend first? If you won't listen to the teacher, then listen to your mother: Good moms never tell their kids to keep things inside. Let close supporters in on what's eating you. Otherwise, there's a price to pay for silence, and these fees may be collected at the lectern. Be smart. Privately talk out the toxin of fear so that it doesn't poison your public speaking efforts. Ironically, disclosing fears will weaken them, not you, and turn you into a more courageous speaker.

IV

Managing Content

28

Follow Your Bliss

JOSEPH CAMPBELL POPULARIZED THE ADVICE "FOLLOW your bliss." Offered as life guidance by this expert on mythology, the saying applies equally well to public speaking. The heart of the tactic is simple: Come up with things you want to share so badly that—despite any fears about public speaking—you just *have* to say them. The moment to speak then becomes an opportunity, not a burden. You have a soapbox, things you're dying to say, and a captive audience. What could be better? It's a match made in speechmaking heaven.

Honoring this principle in speech class, I've learned a lot about topics not typical for my background: hip-hop, tattoos, scrapbooking, skateboarding, mixed martial arts, social networking sites, massive multiplayer online games, and why graffiti should be protected by the First Amendment, to name a few. I want students to enjoy the process of preparing and presenting speeches. If I force them to talk about euthanasia or capital punishment, that will never happen. So, if a class member idolizes the New York Yankees, I hear an informative speech about the New York Yankees — for the twenty-seventh time. After all, who wants to hear a talk by someone who doesn't care about his or her own topic?

You face a tougher job when someone else chooses a topic for you. Bosses, teachers, and speaker-selection committees routinely exercise this privilege. To enliven secondhand material, personalize your talk with firsthand stories and insights. Explore the crossroads where your life and the topic intersect. Dig down deep and unearth facts, examples, statistics, and testimony that excite you. Stash these presents under the Christmas tree. Leave the audience Easter eggs. Sprinkle Hanukkah gelt among the passages. In other words, move from bliss to bliss within your speech. Listeners will experience your genuine excitement during these moments as heartfelt gifts.

Thinking back over private talks that I've shared with students before their speeches, many of the most well-received topics initially haunted speakers with fear, dread, or even a sense of shame. One such student dressed like Charlie Chaplin from head to toe and waddled into class twirling the silent film star's signature cane as an attention-getter. A Muslim student from Kosovo wore a hijab into class and spoke about her firsthand encounters with prejudice. Wanting to be seen as credible advocates, other courageous men and women revealed their sexual orientation while championing social tolerance in persuasive speeches. Presentations such as these stand out among the many thousands that I've heard. Heartfelt candor is always riveting and memorable, whatever hues of the values spectrum shine through your talk.

Remember this simple advice in closing: Any topic will seem interesting if the speaker is interested. Don't fret over finding the perfect crowd-pleasing topic. Open your heart and take a risk. Audiences respond warmly to authenticity, not safe, paint-by-the-numbers speaking formulas. Let your heart choose a topic and then let your mind organize it. Follow your bliss. Put your kite up in the wind. You have a right to pursue happiness, even at the lectern.

29

Your Voice Is Unique

I N 1943, SINGER NAT KING COLE, FATHER OF NATALIE
Cole, released a single called "There Will Never Be Another
You." This voices an extraordinary truth for speakers. Think
about it. There has never been and there will never be another
you. Even science and technology can't change that. Cloning
doesn't produce a carbon copy of a living thing—no experiment with mammals has yet produced an offspring with a history
or life span exactly like its "parent." Dolly the cloned sheep lived
only half as long as others of her kind. Identical twins aren't
identical, either. You would think that if one twin were extraverted, his or her sibling would be, too. But research indicates
odds of less than fifty-fifty for this. A Duke University study
also revealed that—because of lifestyle and environmental influences, called *epigenetics*—there is just a 40 percent chance that
when one identical twin develops Alzheimer's disease, the other
will as well.[1]

Just how unique are you, anyway? First off, your voice is
one of a kind. Blue-chip companies such as JPMorgan Chase

trust their fate to voice-recognition security systems. NASA teamed up with Xerox and developed voice-recognition software for astronauts on space missions. But there's a bigger picture. Go online and check out worldpopclock.com for a second-by-second calculation of our planet's rising human population. You will discover that over seven billion human beings inhabit the earth right now. Beyond that, Carl Haub, senior demographer at the Population Reference Bureau in Washington, D.C., estimates that 108 billion human beings have lived since the advent of our species. Yet in this vast tapestry of human life, you still stand out as a unique, singular thread.

Why is this relevant for speakers? When you relate your own stories, perspectives, and experiences, you can't possibly be wrong. You are the world's expert on yourself. Who from the audience can stand up and say, "That never happened to you," or "No, that's not how you really think or feel"? Take advantage of this authoritative angle and waterproof your speeches by personalizing them. While respecting the need for objective data—particularly in matters that affect decision making—your distinctive slant on a topic may be just as valuable and interesting to an audience as a litany of impersonal research.

Tracing back the roots of speech anxiety among students, I've also learned that many are terrified of the *b* word—*boring*—fearing that classmates will find their turn at the lectern dull. But your personal involvement with the issue under discussion gives a living face to once lifeless subject matter. Whether the topic is box turtles or stock trading, I've seen time and time again that an audience will care because you care. Listeners will be touched because you have been touched. Walking through the gateway nudged open by your curiosity, listeners will gratefully follow in your footsteps and explore a new world.

No matter how far back in time we go, there has never been another person with your exact physical, emotional, and intellectual makeup. And no matter how far forward into the future we travel, the same will hold true. You are it. You are the one-time expression of an unrepeatable living creature. Life filters through each of us differently, so if you have one-of-a-kind ideas and perspectives to share with the human community, you are the only person who can do it. Because people throughout history have valued and voiced the unique messages they carry, such as the dream of Dr. Martin Luther King Jr., the world is a better place. Don't sell yourself short. No other human being can ever see or say what's inside you. Take some time to clear your throat, and then sing your special song to the rooftops of the world.

30

Choose Your Words Wisely

FOR BETTER OR WORSE, WORDS RATTLE DOWN THE END-less corridors of history. Consider the final words of Comtesse deVercellis. Moments before dying in 1728, she passed gas and uttered this pedestrian wisdom to French philosopher Jean-Jacques Rousseau, who kept vigil at her bedside: "Good, a woman who can fart is not dead." Although a gifted writer herself, this vaporous remark has trailed behind her as a legacy for nearly three hundred years.

If, like many presenters, you're worried about how an audience will respond to what you say, then choose what you say wisely. There is cause for concern on two accounts. First, vocabulary usage significantly shapes audience perceptions of speaker credibility. Second, words are the clothes that your ideas wear. Without suitable attire, they may never gain entrance into the hearts and minds of your listeners.

But where do you start? The dictionary and thesaurus beckon from that dust-laden bookshelf. According to a joint Google/Harvard University project, the English language now boasts over one million words, up from roughly 500,000 in the early 1900s, so reference works are sorely needed. In the midst of this meteoric rise, however, *Utne Reader* reported that since about 1950 the average vocabulary of an American teenager has plummeted from 25,000 to 10,000 words. Like OMG, ROFL, TTYL, what could account for that? Literacy careens down a slippery gadget-strewn slope in America. A recent National Endowment for the Arts survey revealed that today's average book buyer stops reading by page eighteen.[2]

Some of my students' errors announce this trend like flashing red beacons. Witness the speech on the importance of scheduling an annual "mommagram," the auto-crash fatality statistics from "*Carnage*-Mellon University," and the scrappy resistance fighters who resorted to "Mazel Tov" cocktails. Still not convinced? Behold the quote attributed to Sallie Mae, the corporation that underwrites student loans, as if "Sallie" were a real person; the informative speech on "Post-*Dramatic* Stress Disorder"; and the cooking demonstration featuring pancakes prepared on a hot "girdle." Nothing will riddle your credentials faster or redden cheeks quicker than such amateurish gaffes. If you do your homework—which most of my students do—there's just no excuse. Online reference sites such as dictionary.com both spell and pronounce words. Well-read friends, relatives, and teachers can also offer assistance.

Beyond aiding your credibility, words determine how clear, memorable, and powerful a speech will be. Attributed to novelist Gustave Flaubert, the French expression *le mot juste* posits a precise word for every meaning that we wish to convey. Was Malcolm X a "militant extremist" or a "political reformer"? Will global climate change "alter" or "destroy" life as we know it? Each word states and suggests—denotes and connotes—a different meaning, so each word and procession of words will take your listeners on a different journey. Choose accordingly. As Mark Twain wrote to author George Bainton in 1888, "the difference between the *almost right* word and the *right* word is really a large matter — 'tis the difference between the lightning-bug and the lightning."

A single word or phrase can also establish the tone and theme of a speech. The mantra-like recurrence of "I have a dream" — repeated nine times in some form in Dr. King's famous speech — stirred hope in the souls of his listeners. Echoing this optimism in a campaign promise, the word "hope" catapulted then-senator Barack Obama into the White House as president. As these examples suggest, words not only sound notes of meaning but also strike chords of emotion. They influence how listeners frame and feel about your topic. In that regard, author and literary critic Kenneth Burke wrote of "god" and "devil" terms, words so powerful they circumvent reasoning and elicit primal responses. *Blood. Sex. Love. Death.* Such words tunnel through the cerebral cortex and burrow their way into the limbic system. Activist Candace Lightner, for example, coined the acronym MADD — Mothers Against Drunk Driving — powerfully crystallizing the righteous anger of parents who lose their children to intoxicated motorists.

Great speakers know that language is music, too. The sound, lilt, and cadence of words can delight the ear, so savvy presenters will touch the minds and hearts of listeners through their discourse. To do so, be familiar with words and the techniques designed for their elegant usage. Assonance, alliteration, consonance, near rhyme, and onomatopoeia — number these among your new friends. If you believe that laboring over such prosodic choices is tedious or trivial, consider this: If Patrick Henry had declared, "Give me freedom or give me oblivion!" rather than "Give me liberty or give me death!" or if Abraham

Lincoln had intoned "Eighty-seven years ago in July of 1776" instead of "Four score and seven years ago," would we remember their speeches? Speech-writing is a highly paid profession for good reason—words do matter.

Let's return now to practical matters. Selecting words with care will boost your confidence and chances for success as a speaker. Since words can fail us during anxious moments, however, sprinkle key terms from your speech into an outline. Pepper them into your slideshow. Splash them across your tongue like good wine while rehearsing. During a menial, part-time job before entering graduate school, I read *Webster's New World College Dictionary* from cover to cover. When possible, I worked each new word into a sentence and into a conversation. Do the same with unfamiliar words from an upcoming presentation. While you don't need to remember *stromuhr*, *cymotrichous*, or *guetapens*—winning words in recent National Spelling Bees—keep the central thoughts of your talk poised at the tip of your tongue.

The muse of language now beckons. Drag out the dictionary and thesaurus. Blow off the dust. Scroll through those shimmering entries on your computer screen. Befriend words. Embrace them shamelessly. Let words seduce you and slip under your skin. While the Comtesse de Vercellis could not exercise verbal discretion on her deathbed, you still have your wits about you. A *speech*? Nothing more than words followed by more words. Choose their company wisely.

31

Select Ideas That Support You

LIKE A NOVICE CHESS PLAYER SQUARING OFF AGAINST A grand master, the anxious speaker can feel like a lone pawn defending his king against a marauding army of mounted knights. Defeat seems inevitable. While chess and public speaking differ in many respects, in a strategic sense ideas *do* form the rank and file of your rhetorical army. Choose each foot soldier wisely and your banner will fly over the battlements in victory; choose poorly and barbarian hordes will sweep through your ranks.

But how do you select ideas wisely as a presenter? As a speech professional who instructs, critiques, and coaches, I can offer five anxiety-reducing guidelines: Your ideas should be accurate, clear, original, on-point, and engaging. Let's take a brief look at each.

If your ideas aren't accurate, your credibility as a speaker will flutter like a tattered flag. Whether intentional deception—think cyclist Lance Armstrong denying doping allegations—or hapless ignorance—think public figures denying that the Holocaust ever occurred—your presentation is only as strong as its weakest idea. Check facts. Check again. If you roam the Internet, tiptoe cautiously through this red-light district of seductive misinformation. Mine the "invisible Web," that vast portion of the Internet that contains a mother lode of high-grade information not indexed by popular search engines.[3] Your local, county, state, and college libraries pay for subscriptions to these online databases. As sister efforts of Project Gutenberg, the first collection of free e-books, both books.google.com and scholar.google.com house millions of scholarly works.

Next, if your ideas aren't clear, the audience won't understand you. Four simple strategies can help. First, define key terms, particularly when discussing scientific or technical material. If you speak about RAM but don't mention Random Access Memory, some poor soul will believe that bighorn sheep work for Microsoft. Second, as mentioned elsewhere, use terms correctly. Stumbling over words will confuse the audience and tarnish your speaking persona, as when a former student solemnly referred to Nazi Germany's vast network of "consternation camps." Third, although simple strategies, signposting (using "first," "second," and "third" to announce main points) and parallel construction aid with clarity. Julius Caesar famously illustrated parallel construction: "I came. I saw. I conquered." There is little room for confusion. Finally, illustrate abstract concepts with concrete examples. Plato offered the analogy of an urn to illustrate the shortcomings of language: Communicating the ideas we have in mind, he wrote, is like smashing an urn and then asking a listener to reassemble its pieces, each word representing a shattered fragment of the once-whole vessel. The chance of a perfect reconstruction is slim, so put the odds in your favor by clearly tracing out the contours of your ideas.

Our third word to the wise: Always present original material. In my experience, speakers who plagiarize typically appear nervous, avoid eye contact, mispronounce unfamiliar words, and adopt unnatural speaking cadences when delivering pilfered material. While few would load a barbecue grill into their pickup truck without paying, words in the form of songs, plays, poems, articles, speeches, and books tempt some like unguarded jewels. But U.S. and international copyright laws protect such creations, and stolen property is stolen property — whether physical or intellectual. Even the Girl Scouts were warned about singing "Happy Birthday" around the campfire — Warner Music Group owns the song's copyright. And former Beatle George Harrison was successfully sued by the publisher of "He's So Fine" over the melody of Harrison's 1970 hit "My Sweet Lord." No one is immune from prosecution. Meanwhile, back at the podium, I've seen many a presenter turn red-faced when an audience member questioned the source of supposedly original material. Why take that risk and ratchet up your angst?

Fourth, on-point ideas that support your speaking purpose are a must given the shrinking attention span of today's audiences. History offers an instructive example. Even with his languid eastern-Kentucky accent, Abraham Lincoln took just two-and-a-half minutes to deliver the Gettysburg Address. Nonetheless, it is chiseled in Indiana limestone on the Lincoln Memorial for future generations to ponder. As the top-billed attraction of the dedication ceremony at Gettysburg, renowned nineteenth-century orator Edward Everett spoke for two-and-a-half hours. Lincoln was a footnote on the program that day; Everett is now a footnote in American history. The quality of your ideas — not their quantity or length — generates rhetorical power.

Finally, choose supporting material that engages an audience. The Brooklyn Bridge is 5,989 feet long? Ho-hum.

Engineer John A. Roebling, the designer of the bridge, was so tough that he had his crushed toes amputated without an anesthetic? Now you've got my attention. Smoking causes emphysema? Yawn. Smoking cigarettes leads to impotence? Sweat breaks on my brow. If wondering about their relative power, communication researchers note that stories captivate, persuade, and linger longer in memory than other forms of supporting material.[4]

According to the Federal Trade Commission, over 30,000 radio and broadcast television stations beamed signals across the United States in 2012. There were also 644 million active Web sites in the world during that same time period, according to Netcraft, an Internet research and security company. Unlike the soapbox orator of the 1800s, when a modern presenter stands to speak he or she is just one of over a half billion signals that can stream into a listener's world.

Nonetheless, good speakers still draw crowds. On January 21, 2013, over a million spectators packed the National Mall in Washington, D.C., to hear President Barack Obama deliver his second inaugural address. Like other top-notch presenters, you can cut through the inner and outer static that competes with your ideas by crafting clear, accurate, original, on-point, and engaging material. Returning to our chess match analogy, winning rhetorical moves lie within your grasp. Choose ideas strategically and you will decisively capture the audience's attention. As French novelist and playwright Victor Hugo observed, "An invasion of armies can be resisted, but not an idea whose time has come."

32

Snap the Pieces into Place

J UST AS CHOOSING WORDS AND IDEAS WISELY WILL IN-
crease your self-assurance, so will assembling the right pieces
into the introduction, body, and conclusion of your presentation. How does one do that? Wait, breaking news just crossed
the wire . . .

*Astronomers from Harvard University announced today that they have
accurately deciphered the ancient Mayan calendar. On the evening of the
next summer solstice, Asteroid Armageddon will scorch through our atmosphere and vaporize planet earth. Don't despair! If you keep listening, I'll
reveal where to board an interplanetary spaceship, the ideal type of rocket
on which to embark, and the most hospitable new worlds to inhabit. How
do I know this? Besides working as a speech professor, I hold PhDs in
Astronomy from both MIT and Princeton University, with world-renowned
expertise in rogue asteroids. If you want to survive, please listen carefully.*

That last campy paragraph houses the essential elements
of a speech introduction: an attention-getter, reason to listen, credibility statement, and preview of the main ideas. After an attention-getter lures in audience members, you must

satisfactorily answer three questions to maintain their interest: What topic and ideas will you speak about? Why should they care about that subject matter? And why should they believe what you have to say? This last question demands a credibility statement highlighting your research, education, experience, and accomplishments vis-à-vis the topic.

What about the stuff in the middle, the body of the presentation? Constructing a talk is like putting together a puzzle. Simply find the edge pieces and work your way back into the middle. When eyeballing a speech, these borders are the introduction and conclusion, which lay out and then restate your thesis. The body then supplies key structural pieces that bridge together the opening and closing of your talk.

Whether you speak for five minutes or an hour, some general rules apply to the inner core of a talk:

- Develop two to five main points.
- Begin and end with strong points.
- Balance the time addressing main ideas.
- Illustrate abstract concepts with concrete examples.
- Link points together with transitional words and phrases.
- Be sure to support your ideas.

A few words of advice about the importance of support: Engaged audience members will silently challenge you with "How come?" "Says who?" and "Prove it!" If delivering an informative talk, offer ample supporting material to illustrate your ideas. If a persuasive spiel, bolster your claims with solid evidence and sound reasoning. New York Yankee Derek Jeter is a closet Rastafarian? Please cite more than *Wikipedia* as proof. The more novel or controversial your claims, the more credible should be the facts, examples, statistics, and testimony marshaled as support.

As you work your way in from the edges of the puzzle, use one pattern of organization for main points and other patterns, as appropriate, for sub-points. A spatial scheme could map out major Renaissance artists by their native countries while a chronological pattern might trace back each painter's life story. Surprise within the structure of patterns. You might, for example, compare the Madonnas of Michelangelo, Titian, and Raphael and then explore how each artist's background influenced his interpretation of the same subject matter. I've listened to speeches for seventeen years, yet I still take delight in the novel and nuanced structural variations that speakers invent.

Hang on—another Reuters news flash just heated up the wire! *To escape from Asteroid Armageddon, immediately make for an embarkation point at Cape Canaveral, the Cosmodrome in Kazakhstan, or Wenchang, China. Choose your spaceship carefully. Don't board a rickety Soyuz rocket; only a retrofitted space shuttle travels at sufficient velocity to escape earth's atmosphere and boldly encounter new worlds. Flee now! Save yourself! Save your children! Ensure the future of humanity!*

And there you have it: a summary, call for action, and memorable closing—the essential elements of a conclusion, in this case for a persuasive talk. In brief, when a speech winds down listeners want to hear the main points in a nutshell, a clear-cut course of action if needed, and a distinct yet artful signal that the presentation is ending. An old expression about speechmaking, often attributed to British prime minister Winston Churchill, describes the journey from preview through main points to review: "Tell them what you're going to tell them, then tell them, then tell them what you just told them."

Public speaking is the art of skillfully gaining, holding, and releasing the attention of an audience. Consequently, the beginnings and endings of talks require special care. According to primacy-recency theory, your first and last encounters with a person, place, or thing are most memorable and determine your overall impression. Do not the beginnings and endings of love affairs burn most brightly on the page and the screen? Likewise, the takeoff and landing of your relationship with an audience demands artful consideration. Don't jilt the affections of listeners by fumbling at the outset or parting clumsily. Some traditional options for opening and closing include stories, quotations, humor, startling statements, rhetorical questions, and references to the audience, occasion, or setting. Use these same rhetorical devices to regain attention that wanes during the body of the speech.

The landing wheels are down. The seatbelt sign is off. My sincere apologies to learned passengers who lunged for air sickness bags during the preceding interplanetary flight. Yes, this chapter is a simplification of speech structure. Yes, readers should seek out a full treatment in a reputable speech textbook. But I swear by Jay Leno's chin, there is truth in caricature. Speech anxiety reduces complex cognitions to a Morse code of catchwords and phrases, so a simple SOS of essential speech features can aid apprehensive learners. With that noble intention declared, I've snapped the final piece of this simple speechmaking portrait into place.

33

Familiarize, Don't Memorize

W HEN I WAS A KID IN GRAMMAR SCHOOL, JUST AFTER
dinosaurs died out, students had to memorize and recite
important lessons. Multiplication tables, U.S. state capitals, and
the Gettysburg Address were favorite assignments. When your
name was called on the appointed day, you marched to the front
of the classroom, and both the teacher and students gawked as
you muddled through an incoherent version of some famous
passage.

Such rote learning is now passé, but many speakers still revert
to this cumbersome style when preparing speeches. Much of the
pressure and anxiety of public speaking arises from the unrealis-
tic expectation of recalling every word of a talk in its exact order.
American adults typically speak at a rate of 120 to 150 words
per minute. A twenty-minute talk might then entail remembering
up to 3,000 words—more than ten times the length of the Gettysburg Address. If you're keeping track the old-fashioned way,
that's 150 sets of fingers and toes. I'd be scared to death, too, if I
had to remember all that material.

Speech teachers offer a simple alternative for this burdensome chore: Use an extemporaneous speaking style. When it comes to delivery methods, memorization is outdated, manuscripts are typically used by bigwigs only, and a talk of any importance should never be entrusted to an impromptu stream of words and ideas. Extemporaneous speaking is the sane middle ground between desperately winging it and meticulously writing out an entire speech.

What, exactly, is extemporaneous speaking? In a phrase—familiarize, don't memorize. Familiarize yourself with the flow of words and ideas in your talk rather than committing every syllable to heart. The advantages are legion. Primarily, you can observe and adapt to audience reactions while giving yourself permission to cut out, reword, and even invent new material on the fly. Although your skeletal outline will remain intact, you can flesh out each budding limb and digit as the moment demands. Jazz legend Miles Davis captured the beauty of extemporaneous performances with this advice: "Do not fear mistakes—there are none." Like jazz improvisation, your words will flow out differently each time with extemporaneous speaking, yet you will still convey the same message—on key.

For you unbelievers, extemporaneity does require an act of faith—faith in your own ability to recall information and form sentences. But you do this every day in every conversation, don't you? Public speakers, repeat this mantra after me: "Be extemporaneous!" If you can't decipher what seems like ancient Sanskrit, here are four other ways to understand the concept: Being extemporaneous means that you use a conversational style of speaking, practice without over-rehearsing your speech, choose the exact wording of your ideas the moment that you say them, and respond to the inspiration of the moment without losing your way. Heck, that last one even sounds like fun.

The takeaway lesson from this chapter is simple: Talk to the audience; don't recite. You have been asked to do public speaking, not perform a memory feat. The former is an art form admired by many successful adults; the latter is a chore still hated by schoolchildren the world over.

34

You Must Remember This

Aᴿ ꜰᴇᴡ ʏᴇᴀʀꜱ ʙᴀᴄᴋ ᴀ Tᴇxᴀꜱ ᴍᴀɴ ɢᴏᴛ ᴍᴀʀʀɪᴇᴅ, ᴅɪꜱᴀᴘ-peared just before his honeymoon, and was found wandering three days later near an abandoned motel. After six years of courtship, Sean McNulty couldn't recognize his new bride — or his mother. An odd case of amnesia had clamped off his memories like an unforgiving tourniquet. This story illustrates what speakers fear most: standing in the stage lights with an utterly blank mind and unblinking eyes staring at them.

I don't say this arbitrarily. A Canadian study found that 74 percent of respondents fear their minds will go blank during a speech. Another four-year study of 1,617 students at Brookdale Community College revealed that speakers most frequently identify the fear of forgetting as their chief concern.[5] Since the point of making a speech is to share ideas, it does present a bit of a problem if you can't recall them. Forget about this concern for the moment. Leave that stack of Post-it notes on your desk. Untie that string from your finger. Let's take a quick trip down memory lane and visit four proven techniques that stave off forgetfulness.

To start off, patterns of organization offer a low-tech solution to forgetting that should be in every speaker's toolkit. Although more than a dozen patterns exist, presenters commonly use five: chronological, spatial, topical, causal, and problem-solution. Suppose, for example, that you will give a presentation about the Taj Mahal, the beautiful seventeenth-century Indian monument. If you first speak about the gardens and reflecting pool outside the main buildings and then speak about the design of the complex, moving from the ground floor up to the minarets, a spatial pattern would map out your ideas. You can also use patterns of organization to arrange sub-points. A chronological pattern, for example, could block out minor points by recounting how each design element of the Taj Mahal evolved over time. Whatever pattern you choose, presenting a quilt work of ideas rather than ragged scraps of thought will help both you and your audience to follow and retain your points.

Next, let's revisit a technique that you first learned in grammar school. Can you recall the five Great Lakes? The colors of the rainbow? The notes on the lines of the treble clef? If you used the memory aids HOMES, Roy G. Biv, or "Every good boy does fine," you certainly can. Acronyms, as you know, are words formed by combining the initial letters of a series of words. Creating sentences with the first letter of a group of words is a close cousin. Students remember the order of operations in math—parentheses, exponents, multiplication, addition, and subtraction—with the offbeat sentence "Please excuse my dear Aunt Sally." Don't underestimate the value of these everyday strategies. Acronyms save lives. The American Red Cross's CPR guidelines, ABC (airway, breathing, circulation), and the steps for using a fire extinguisher, PASS (pull, aim, squeeze, sweep), are summed up by acronyms. If acronyms work under life-and-death circumstances, simple memory aids can certainly help out during the stress of a speech.

Moving back in time, ancient orators developed the Roman room method as a mnemonic system. In this approach, a speaker associates the ideas of a speech with the places in his or her home. The first idea of the speech is linked to the first place in your home, say the foyer. The second idea of the speech would be linked to the next place in your house, perhaps the hallway, and so on, until you finish a mental tour of your home, thereby completing your speech.[6]

Let's assume, for example, that you will do an informative talk about emerging trends in social media. If the first point in your presentation is a story about Mark Zuckerberg, you might picture the CEO of Facebook hanging on a coat hook in the foyer of your home. This silly image will help you to recall your opening idea. If a speech is particularly long and you run out of rooms, simply walk out of your house and down the street, associating each new idea with landmarks around your neighborhood. The Roman room method is the ancient origin of our modern expressions "in the first place," "in the second place," and so forth.

A final tool at your disposal is the key-word outline. Since a manuscript is cumbersome and unnecessary for most speaking occasions, a brief key-word outline of your major points will usually suffice. These outlines are easy to construct. Rather than writing out full sentences, simply post salient words and phrases that correspond with major ideas in your talk's introduction, body, and conclusion. With a quick glance, these easy-to-read signposts will remind you of all the stops along your speaking journey.

As public speaking goes, one fundamental thing still applies: You won't recall what you don't organize. Each of these four memory aids reduces thousands of spoken words into a few logically arranged points. Each also forces you to think about your material, which will aid with natural memory. If you're still worried about recalling ideas, you can even combine techniques. Choose a suitable pattern of organization, arrange your ideas in a key-word outline, create an acronym spelling out your main points, and then nest these ideas in your home using the Roman room method. As Samuel Johnson, author of *A Dictionary of the English Language*, noted some two hundred years ago, "The true art of memory is the art of attention." By taking the time to connect the dots before a speech, the big picture will stay with you during a speech, and that will help you to breathe easier at the lectern.

35

Visual Aids Can Be an Ally

VISUAL AIDS CAN FORM A POWERFUL LINE OF DEFENSE against speech anxiety. If you're feeling nervous, key thoughts plastered on slides or poster boards will jump-start your sputtering mind. If you're feeling shy, some of the audience's attention will be directed away from you and onto the visual aid. If you lingered at the concession stand while they passed out the gift of gab, well-crafted visual aids will invite favorable audience judgments based on something other than your words. If presenting in a language other than your native tongue, visual aids can clarify ideas for audience members confused by accents or inaccurate pronunciations. Finally, ennobled by the pageantry of visual aids, an otherwise run-of-the-mill presentation can create a larger-than-life impression.

With all these alluring benefits, you might want to grab your magic markers and construction paper right now. Before sitting down at the workbench or keyboard, however, let's review some common pitfalls of visual aid use. Watching countless presentations in academic and business settings has painfully etched some of these transgressions into my mind. Why not learn from my suffering and avoid your own?

First and foremost, don't stare at your visual aids! The most frequent error I see among beginning speakers is limited eye contact. All those lovely, tempting words splashed across a nearby surface may seem like a godsend, but ogling them will only damage your credibility and connection with the audience. Glance occasionally at visual aids to stay on track, but give the audience the lion's share of your attention.

Second, post only key words or phrases in your slides and on poster boards. The more text crammed into your visual aids, the more competition you create for yourself and the less needed you seem as a speaker. Serve up text as hors d'oeuvres—whet the audience's appetite, but leave them wanting more.

Third, on a related theme, if using presentation software, don't torture listeners by inserting the full text of your speech into a slideshow and then reading it. Colleges typically offer courses in public speaking, not public reading.

A fourth common problem among speakers is poorly constructed visual aids. You've had all the time in the world before your talk to prepare them, so in this one area the audience can expect perfection. Sloppy layouts, unreadable fonts, and faulty grammar, spelling, or punctuation torpedo professionalism. Your presentation will be judged in the context of your handiwork, so unless you craft top-notch visual aids, don't bother to use them.

A fifth problem that besets presenters is inadequate rehearsal. You don't want a "pay no attention to that man behind the curtain" moment during your presentation. In one classroom demonstration speech, a student tugged so hard on a package of cake mix that it exploded and rained down white flour on his head. Scissors would have been a good idea. To avoid such mishaps, practice until you are familiar with both the content and mechanics of your visual aids.

Finally, even when you practice with visual aids, nature and technology don't always cooperate when the curtain rises. Think of your worst-case scenario and then brainstorm backup plans. What will you do if your slides don't work? A key video clip malfunctions? The laser pointer fails? Savvy presenters often finesse these awkward moments with humor and ad-lib solutions. When her CD player went belly-up during a salsa-dancing demonstration, a student asked the class to clap out the rhythm of the dance. The audience had a great time, and the presenter still achieved her speaking purpose.

In closing, it's no accident that movies, television, video games, and the Internet have mushroomed in popularity. Human beings love visual stimulation. In fact, most people prefer visual over aural learning—we're just hardwired that way. As visual literacy expert Mary Alice White observed, "People learn more than half of what they know from visual information."

If called for, then, why deny audience members the stimulation and yourself the support of appropriate visual aids? Unlike mercurial audience reactions and topsy-turvy speechday emotions, you have complete control over the construction of visual aids. Well-crafted or well-chosen charts, graphs, maps, models, photos, objects, film clips, poster boards, or slideshows can engage the audience and make public speaking a less anxious affair for you.

Time now to get out the glue and scissors. But don't make a mess—make a masterpiece!

36

Use Mental Rehearsal

AS HARRIED WORKERS, PARENTS, AND STUDENTS KNOW, America is a very busy nation. We spend more time on the job each week and enjoy fewer days off each year than citizens in most industrialized nations. Some enrollees in my classes are students, workers, *and* parents, so burning up large chunks of free time to rehearse speeches just isn't in the cards for them. At the same time, however, the fear of forgetting material is a major concern for many speakers. Fortunately, a simple solution called mental rehearsal will address this and other challenges for novice and experienced presenters alike.

An unusual tale crystallizes the power of this strategy. In 1977, Russian dissident Natan Sharansky was arrested by the KGB, the Soviet secret police. A so-called "refusenik"—a Jew denied permission to emigrate from Russia—the Soviet Union convicted him of spying for the United States. This Cold War offense landed Sharansky in Soviet prisons and Siberian labor camps for nine years, including a year of torture and solitary confinement. Rather than despairing during this brutal ordeal, the young computer engineer sorted out his philosophy of life and played chess against himself in his mind. In 1996, without ever having been ranked by the World Chess Federation, Sharansky defeated reigning world champion Garry Kasparov in a simultaneous chess exhibition—all from expertise honed during mental rehearsal.

Distilled from the confluence of performance psychology, guided imagery, and meditation practices, the power of mental rehearsal is affirmed by scores of university studies and anecdotes. After the U.S. women's soccer team won the gold medal in the 2012 Summer Olympics, for example, midfielder Carli Lloyd, who scored both goals in the 2–1 victory over Japan, was asked if she had ever dreamt about such victorious moments while playing soccer as a young girl. Without breaking stride, Lloyd said, "Yes, it's all in the mind," underscoring the importance of visualization in her success as a professional athlete.

Mental rehearsal, often called *visualization*, requires just a few simple steps. First, ease into a relaxed state of mind; second, vividly imagine yourself carrying out an activity with effortless skill; and third, feel the joy and confidence that naturally accompany such success. Not only are you *doing* well, you are also *feeling* good about your top-notch deeds. Think it, do it, then feel it. This practice routine addresses the cognitive, behavioral, and emotional dimensions of performance. Be sure to engage all relevant senses during mental rehearsal. What do you hear, feel, and touch during your talk? If any part of an activity seems fuzzy in your mind's eye, replay the tape until it shifts into focus.

Like a movie director overseeing several camera crews during a film shoot, you can also run through your presentation from multiple viewpoints. Take a step back and imagine the audience's point of view along with your own. What do you look and sound like from a listener's chair? Is your message clear? Would your words and ideas persuade you? At times, I conjure up a hostile crowd and imagine how they might react as compared to a more sympathetic group. Like test-marketing a summer blockbuster, such audience analysis allows you to strategically shift content before uttering a word. If needed, imagine yourself fielding questions after your talk, too. Pose both easy and challenging hypothetical queries so that the actual question-and-answer session will flow smoothly.

I make frequent use of mental rehearsal when preparing talks. When my older brother passed away, for instance, I prepared a eulogy in his honor. Gathering friends for a live practice session was out of the question, since I was traveling out of state. After sketching out a key-word outline, I rehearsed in my mind's eye on the plane, driving on California's highways, and sitting on the mist-shrouded cliffs of Big Sur. Along with conjuring up each part of the talk, I repeated sections of the eulogy aloud to capture both the feel and cadence of key passages. This process seeded natural, organic changes which were then reflected in an evolving key-word outline. When it came time to speak, I felt at ease, connected with the audience, and shared reminiscences from the heart. Although a life filled with memorable events inspired my brother's eulogy, his eulogy was never rehearsed before a live audience. (After my remarks, the funeral director confided that he hadn't heard a more moving tribute during his twenty-seven years in the funeral business.)

In summary, the benefits of mental rehearsal are fivefold: It will enhance your memory, guide content choice, boost your actual performance, motivate you towards a positive outcome, and reduce your anxiety through familiarity with an imagined audience—all without saying a word. Rather than fretting over a grim doomsday scenario, happily envision the glories of your speech-day success. Hoist the trophy. Hear the roar of the crowd. Stand on the gold-medal podium. Since the machinery of the mind can indeed influence future performances, let its ever-rumbling gears and cogwheels aid rather than hinder your creative efforts.

V

Stepping onto the Podium

37

People Want You to Succeed

A CHILLY ASSUMPTION OFTEN LINGERS BELOW THE FEAR of public speaking. Many speakers believe an audience expects perfection and will greet anything less than a stellar performance with hostility. Public speaking is not *American Idol*. Audience members are not judges waiting for you to slip up so they can drench your scorecard with red ink.

After sitting in hundreds of classes while grading thousands of presentations, I can confidently say there is nothing more painful — for both audience and instructor — than watching someone self-destruct at the lectern. A nearly reverential stillness falls over the room when students witness a classmate struggle. Even the bored-since-I-was-born, nothing-really-gets-to-me crowd musters up a few drops of mercy. No one likes to see a comrade fall in the trenches.

When you stand up to speak, realize that people want you to succeed. If you are enrolled in a speech class or presenting at a meeting or conference where peers will also give talks, there is an even greater pool of empathy. These kindred spirits understand your vulnerability firsthand. You are all in the same boat, just sitting at different oars. In addition, speakers often have a long-distance circle of supporters who hold them in their thoughts or prayers. Remember, these folks are rooting for you, too.

Now, some of you may be thinking, "Take off the rose-colored glasses, McDermott! There are people in this world who like to hurt others." Of course there are, and they show up every day in the headlines. But they are exceptions to the civil majority, the often silent multitude that allows society to function. Temper your raw cynicism with some raw data. First, the prevalence of empathy, the capacity to feel for others, is actually quite high in the general population. The National Altruism Study, sponsored by the University of Chicago, found that over 70 percent of respondents reported they *often* have "tender, concerned feelings" for less fortunate people.[1] Second, those who have no feelings for others or take pleasure in witnessing pain are a small minority. Only a few sick souls go to the circus hoping that the trapeze artist slips up. These are sociopaths suffering from what the *Diagnostic and Statistical Manual of Mental Disorders* (DSM-5) now calls Anti-social Personality Disorder. According to the DSM-5, perhaps 4 percent of the American population qualifies for this designation, even less in other nations. Basic math quickly tells us that in an audience of one hundred, just four members might root against you. And these folks need help. Put your faith in the other ninety-six.

In 1913, on the eve of World War I, American author Eleanor Porter wrote an upbeat novel called *Pollyanna*. The heroine of her story is Pollyanna Whittier, a young orphan who faces adversity with unending cheer. According to *Merriam-Webster's Collegiate Dictionary* her name has come to mean, "a person characterized by irrepressible optimism and a tendency to find good in everything." Adopt Pollyanna's rosy viewpoint at the lectern. Think of your audience as a cheering squad, not a firing squad. If you believe that good will come out of your efforts and the hearts of listeners, it often will.

38

Find Friendly Faces

NOVICE SPEAKERS OFTEN FEEL ANXIOUS WITH A ROOM full of people staring at them. Unless you've performed on stage, a speaking engagement may be the first time that so many people eyeball you at once. To make matters worse, eye contact is required in speech courses and expected in boardrooms and town meeting halls alike. Fortunately, every classroom, meeting chamber, or auditorium has its share of friendly faces. God knows, for whatever reasons, these kind souls light up a room with their friendly smiles. These faces are your islands of tranquility when swimming out on the scary sea of public speaking. Head for them like a drowning person heads for a life ring.

Here's how it works. When you first stand up to speak, notice friendly faces around the room. At least one on the right side, one in the middle, and one on the left side of the room will do for starters. As you speak, look at those faces and you will look at all parts of the room! It's that easy. As you feel more confident, gradually expand your gaze to larger areas of the room, going back to those friendly faces when needed.

Here's another trick. If you have friends, classmates, or co-workers in the audience, ask them to smile at you when you speak. As silly as this sounds, it will help you to feel more confident. Sometimes my students make a pact with each other: "If you smile at me when I speak, I'll smile at you when you speak." It's simple, but it works. Why? When we speak we can feel as vulnerable as children careening down a playground slide for the first time. The beaming smile of a waiting parent can offer needed reassurance. Likewise, the warmth of a friendly face can help you feel more secure when taking the risk of speaking in public.

If you can't find friendly faces in the room, just imagine them. Conjure up your mother, father, spouse, partner, Aunt Rosie, or your kindhearted first-grade teacher. Place these folks in empty seats around the room in your mind's eye. Take the shackles off, and let your imagination run wild. During a speech about Frederick Douglass, why not picture the abolitionist sitting in the front row grinning with approval? What the heck, throw in Harriet Tubman, too. If religious or spiritual beliefs gird your life, pack the rafters with saints, angels, and deities. Don't limit this support to your speaking venue; let your imaginary supporters cheer you on during practice sessions, too. Your imagination stirs up the fear of audience disapproval; why not let it generate the warmth of audience acceptance? (If you have difficulty visualizing the presence of others, one student suggested placing a photograph of a loved or admired person on the lectern next to speaking notes as a backup plan.)

One last thought comes to mind. As we learned earlier, psychologist Carl Jung's work on psychological types laid the basis for the Myers-Briggs Type Indicator® (MBTI). The MBTI is the most trusted and widely used personality test in the world. Introverts and extraverts, according to studies, use differing amounts of facial animation. While extraverts may be more animated, introverts can look very serious—even disapproving—while they raptly take in a speaker's information. So don't be fooled. Those serious faces in the crowd may be your biggest fans.

39

Be Audience-Centered

IN THE EARLY 1900s, ADVERTISERS CONSPIRED TO MAKE the American consumer more self-conscious. Stuart Ewen unravels the threads of this scheme in a fascinating book called *Captains of Consciousness: Advertising and the Social Roots of the Consumer Culture.* Paraphrasing industry documents, Ewen reports that advertisers "attempted to turn the consumer's critical functions away from the product and toward himself." To a saddening degree, the attempt of marketeers to turn the critical faculties of consumers against themselves has succeeded. Perfumes, mouthwashes, and deodorants mask the scents of our bodies. Hair dyes, tooth whiteners, and makeup gloss over our natural features. Taking image-consciousness one step further, American consumers spent over $10 billion in 2011 on cosmetic surgery, according to the American Society for Aesthetic Plastic Surgery. By contrast, UNICEF, the United Nations Children's Fund, operated on a *worldwide* 2012–2013 budget of $966 million. Botox injections trump child welfare by a ten-to-one margin.

Our already acute sense of self-consciousness often heightens during public speaking. There we stand in the spotlight, feeling naked, for all to see. Ordinarily confident people clam up, tremble, and pray to the god of time for swift deliverance. In fact, most of my students dread watching digital recordings of their own speeches. Even in the full bloom of youth, some cannot bear to watch themselves.

Knowing that tensions will run high in a public speaking class, I provide instruction on managing speech anxiety early in the term. I joke with students about what their internal dialogue might sound like while speaking: "Is that spinach stuck between my teeth? Why won't my left eyelid stop twitching? Why does everyone look like they hate me? Only two minutes have gone by—my god! Did I just burp? That guy in the second row will never date me now. I know I will fail this course. I may as well drop the class today. Why did I enroll in college anyway?"

Students soon learn an easy remedy for the crippling habit of self-consciousness: Be audience-centered. What does this mean? Rather than focusing on your fears as a speaker, focus on the needs and perspectives of audience members as listeners. In short, turn the magnifying glass away from yourself and onto the audience. The internal dialogue then shifts: "Can they hear me? Am I going too fast? Too slow? Are they confused? Do they need another example to understand my point?" The adjustments you make while delivering a speech then move away from being *liked* as a person to being *understood* as a speaker. Being accepted by all is an impossible goal; being understood by most is an attainable end.

Let's wax metaphysical for a moment: Adopting a broader view of public address can also help you transcend self-consciousness. First, realize that you speak as a servant of the group. After all, you already know your material, so your message is for the benefit of the audience, not you. Let a sense of social consciousness draw you out and replace the self-consciousness that weighs you down. Second, realize that *synchronicity*— the term coined by psychologist Carl Jung for "meaningful coincidence"—may work through your inspiration. Over the years that I've taught public speaking, students have often unwittingly chosen topics that answer the silent hopes and prayers of classmates. Someone presents a speech about anorexia while a young woman in class struggles with that eating disorder. Someone's mother suffers from cancer and a student delivers a speech about a cutting-edge treatment. One student gives a talk about traveling to Australia as another ponders transferring to an Australian university.

Although I check on student topics and occasionally prune out-of-bounds choices—like the proposed how-to speech on Molotov cocktails—more often than not, I respect the inspiration that led a student to pick a topic. The word *inspire* literally means "to fill with breath or spirit." We can be an instrument through which inspired breath moves. We can be a channel through which helpful messages flow. As the bearers of such glad tidings, it behooves us to push fear out of the way for the sake of our listeners.

Returning to practical considerations, these serendipitous moments occur more often when we keep the audience in mind throughout the speech preparation process. Ask yourself, "What topic might interest this audience? What kinds of examples will seem relevant? What language will they understand? What type of humor—if any—will tickle them?" If you know the audience well enough, you can even share facts and stories drawn from the lives of your listeners. In addition, picture the audience in your mind's eye while practicing. By adopting this strategy, your audience will feel more like a group of friends when you speak than a crowd of strangers.

Unexpected results arise from keeping the audience at center stage during a speech. Paradoxically, the less you focus on yourself while speaking, the better you will do and the more the audience will like you. The less you worry about how the audience *reacts* to you and the more you care about how you *act* towards them, the more they will embrace you. To be remembered, forget yourself. To succeed, put others first. To gain the most, offer your speech as a gift. Indian leader Mahatma Gandhi said it best: "The fragrance always remains on the hand that gives the rose."

40

Harmonize Your Voices

Gᴿᴼˢˢᴵᴺᴳ ᴼᵛᴱᴿ $2.1 ʙᴵʟʟᴵᴼᴺ ᴛᴼ ᴅᴬᵀᴱ ᵂᴼᴿʟᴅᵂᴵᴅᴱ, *Titanic* is the second most commercially successful film ever made. One of the most memorable scenes depicts Leonardo DiCaprio's character, Jack Dawson, leaning over the railing of the mammoth ocean liner, shouting, "I'm the king of the world!" With arms outspread like a bird in flight, Dawson defiantly perches on the ship's bow and howls his proclamation with jumping-out-of-your-skin exuberance. The scene convinces because Jack's words, voice, and body all say the same thing.

In one artfully delivered line, DiCaprio crystallizes a simple yet profound lesson about powerful public speaking: Harmonize your voices. This technique is the nearest thing I can share to a public speaking secret. The gist is simple. You have three "voices": your words, your body, and your actual speaking voice. When each says the same thing, you are most powerful. If you argue that contributing to charities is important, for example, your words, voice, and body all need to convey that message. If your voice trails off as you check the ceiling for cobwebs, the audience won't buy your argument. Every contradiction opens another crack in your ship's hull.

University studies substantiate this observation. Research by Dr. Albert Mehrabian, a pioneer in the field of nonverbal communication, establishes that listeners rely on body language and tone of voice to determine the truth when a speaker's words are contradictory or confusing. How great is this reliance? Listeners derive 93 percent of meaning from nonverbal cues.[2] In other words, how you look, how you behave, and how you say things serve as a living *context* for interpreting the spoken *text* of your message.

What promise does this hold for battling speech anxiety? Presenters usually don't like to seem weak, nervous, or lacking in courage in front of an audience. Feeling nervous is one thing, but looking nervous is quite another. Speakers, however, rarely *say*, "I feel so nervous!"—their voices and bodies give them away. The vocal and physical channels of communication tip a speaker's shaky hand. When used skillfully, harmonizing your voices ends this unconscious betrayal. Through awareness and behavioral fine-tuning, you can simultaneously project a strong, unified speaking persona while delivering a focused, on-point message. In a word, you will look, feel, and sound powerful.

To get the hang of this technique, record your rehearsal sessions or rely on a practice audience to discover if your voices truly coalesce. Look for and request honest feedback. Make sure that all your working parts crank out the same message. Bold words but fidgeting hands, inspired thoughts but a monotonous voice, or dire ultimatums but a questioning tone will undermine your speaking efforts. To scrutinize nonverbal communication, some speakers find it helpful to watch their videos with the sound turned off. The same principle applies, by the way, whether you are standing at a lectern or sitting down in a meeting. Each of our communication channels constantly sends out signals, so monitoring and adjusting these data streams will enhance your overall speaking competence.

A helpful public speaking corollary follows from this simple principle: Never draw attention to a mistake. If you say, "Sorry, I mispronounced that," or "Jeez, I forgot something again," or "How could I be so stupid!" these ad-lib criticisms will undermine your credibility. They also insult listeners who have been taking you seriously. Never create the impression that we're wasting our time by listening to you. After working so hard on your message, why let the messenger — in this case you — ruin it?

In summary, say what you mean, sound like you mean it, and look like you mean it as well. Both the strength of your message and perceived strength as a speaker rely on harmonizing the verbal, vocal, and physical channels of communication. Like the triumvirate, or trio of leaders, that once ruled ancient Rome, let the trio of your words, body, and voice speak out powerfully on your behalf.

41

Practice Deep Breathing

As an undergraduate at Rutgers College, I practiced yoga. One night I lost my balance during a headstand and tumbled over. My bare feet slapped against a windowpane and sent glass cascading onto a concrete walkway two stories below. I wasn't startled when the window broke and, after checking the walkway, finished my yoga routine and cleaned up the shattered glass in the morning. That night, I learned a powerful lesson about the calming power of deep breathing.

Deep breathing is an ancient practice that soothes both mind and body. Breath-control exercises first surfaced in the sacred literature of India and China between 2000 and 3000 BC. In contemporary society, breathing exercises appear in many incarnations. We see the practice in the guise of yoga, meditation, diaphragmatic breathing in voice training, as a stress reduction technique, and as focused breathing in the Lamaze method of natural childbirth.

To understand how deep breathing works, let's begin with a quick lesson in neurophysiology. The autonomic nervous system (ANS) regulates our internal organs and muscles. The ANS has two parts, the sympathetic and parasympathetic nervous systems. The sympathetic nervous system energizes the body for fight-or-flight responses. If a car runs a red light as you step into a crosswalk, glands and organs squirt glucose and adrenaline into your bloodstream, which fuels muscles that whisk you out of the way. The parasympathetic nervous system complements the sympathetic and promotes rest and repose among our organs and muscles. Deep breathing stimulates the parasympathetic and calms down the sympathetic nervous system.

Public speaking becomes a challenge when the sympathetic nervous system gets triggered at a time when we desperately need the services of the parasympathetic system. With our feet nailed to the floor behind a lectern, we become flooded by the red flashing lights and alarm bells of our prehistoric fight-or-flight response. The heart pounds while blood is shunted away from internal organs to mobilize large muscles. Our primitive brain scans the horizon for *T. rex*. Limbs tremble. Words fail us.

Deep breathing short-circuits this ancient survival system. Control of the autonomic nervous system (think "automatic") falls back into our own hands. By regulating your breathing, you—rather than your nerves—govern your heart rate, respiration, and blood pressure. Here's how it works: Instead of taking a deep breath by lifting up your shoulders, simply fill your tummy with air first, letting it distend, and then gradually inflate the rest of your lungs. By pushing your abdomen out, you force down the diaphragm, allowing the lungs to fully expand. Breathe in through your nose to warm and filter the air, then breathe out through your mouth. Don't rush. The longer you continue deep breathing, the slower your pulse and respiration rates, and the calmer you will feel.

It's easy to get caught off guard by the surge of adrenaline that accompanies those first steps to the lectern, so start deep breathing in your seat well before your time to speak. You don't want to gasp for air and choke on your opening lines. Continue to breathe consciously as you speak. Rather than filling up your lungs with air like a big bellows and then squeezing out words until you are breathless, take short breaths between phrases to stay oxygenated. Pause frequently to take in air and to let the audience absorb your message; don't hold out for sentence or paragraph breaks to breathe. Pausing also gives you a chance to check notes and gather your thoughts and can signal a shift in topics or create suspense for the audience at key moments.

Research shows that besides helping public speakers, deep breathing promotes numerous other health benefits. Most impressively, if regulated breathing can help women through childbirth without drugs or surgery, it can certainly help you deliver a speech with dignity and composure.

42

Stay in the Moment

IN THE TALE "A PAINFUL CASE" FROM HIS BOOK OF SHORT stories called *Dubliners*, Irish novelist James Joyce wrote that Mr. Duffy "lived at a little distance from his body." Besieged by turbulent emotions, some speakers also take leave of their senses, fully returning to awareness only after their closing remarks. Such presenters don't clearly recall their words, actions, or audience responses, leaving each speech a jumbled blur in the rearview mirror.

There is a simple cure for this mental flight: Stay in the moment. Staying in the moment permits a speaker to read and respond to the shifting moods and needs of a live audience while remaining composed. From this centered place, the circumference of awareness expands, speaking choices flow more easily, and the verbal and nonverbal signals of a presenter ring with greater authenticity. In other words, being grounded gives a speaker solid ground to stand upon.

When the demands of a presentation or the prospect of a negative outcome feel overwhelming, however, how does a speaker stay in the here and now? An unexpected source suggests an answer. Meditation traditions ask practitioners to focus on the breath or on a mantra, a special word or phrase that is repeated.[3] When attention drifts away, the meditator gently returns awareness back to the breath or sound of the mantra. Similarly, if your mind wanders while speaking, gently return to the moment and task at hand. Don't fret over a forgotten phrase from your introduction—that's behind you. Don't ponder questions the audience might ask later—that's ahead of you. Let the words that you are about to speak be your ever-changing mantra. Stay in the moment and think only of the task before you—that's all you can control. Do each part of your speech well, however, and the whole is done well.

While part of staying in the moment requires reading and responding to a live audience, another aspect is faithfully conveying the ideas that you prepared in advance. If one of my students gets stuck during a speech, typically in the introduction when anxiety runs high, I simply glance down at his or her outline and offer a hint: "I think you might have wanted to give us a preview of your main ideas next." If familiar enough with his or her speaking journey, the student heeds the signpost and begins anew. Along with honoring the nuances of the moment, then, structuring an outline and conducting rehearsals are essential for most successful presentations. Without this preparation, there is no toehold if you slip and no ball of string to lead you back out of the labyrinth.

This pairing of preparation and spontaneity suggests a simple ground rule for effective speaking: Take what you have prepared in the *past* and bring it to life in the *present*. Take things a minute, a moment, or a word at a time if necessary. Just be here now. Even the greatest orator can use only one breath well at a time. The magic of speaking always lies in the present moment, at the ever-changing crossroads where chance and readiness meet. A speaker with presence dwells in that present moment.

Beyond the lectern, staying in the moment is a wonderful life practice. To take notice of your surroundings, be sensitive to others, fully focus on the task at hand, and respond rather than react is a gift for all, whether experienced on or off the podium. And if you can remain present while addressing an audience—a task that so many needlessly fear—you can stay present during much of life. Undertaken in this spirit, public speaking becomes a form of standing meditation, a mindful practice that transforms a mechanical skill into a sublime art.

43

Dress for Speaking Success

Y OU CAN'T CONTROL THE WEATHER, SIZE OF A CROWD,
or alignment of the stars when you speak, but you *do*
exercise complete dominion over your clothing choices. You
must get dressed anyway before a presentation, so why not put
on something that works for you? To invite composure while
speaking, the clothes you wear should be suitable, comfortable,
and able to conceal any outward signs of nervousness. Let's
address these three goals in order.

First, you wouldn't wear a bow tie for a speech on skateboarding or a tee shirt for a financial presentation. Choose
clothing that is suitable for the occasion. As a rule of thumb,
job candidates dress one level above the advertised posi-
tion during an interview. The same holds true for speakers. Whatever the occasion, dress better than your audience.
Gussying up creates the impression that you care about the
event and also conveys professionalism. Keep in mind that
even when you're not speaking, your clothes speak on your
behalf.

Second, it's important to feel comfortable while presenting. Wear attire that doesn't confine your neck, arms, or waist. Belts, clothing, or jewelry that constricts your breathing, circulation, or gesturing won't serve you. For gentlemen in business apparel, buy collared shirts with the neck one size larger than your measurements require. This old-school trick leaves you breathing more easily when sporting a tie. For a casual yet professional look, try a turtleneck or mock turtleneck with a blazer. For women donning business togs, a pantsuit or skirt suit is *de rigueur*. Favor flats or a modest pump over towering high heels when slipping on shoes. Colors? Gray or navy blue with a splash of red in a tie, wrap, or scarf still commands attention. Jewelry? Leave bracelets that might clang against a lectern or oversized sparkly earrings at home. Your wardrobe shouldn't upstage you.

In less formal settings, such as a classroom, dress down, but avoid clothing that is sloppy or in poor taste. Don't take your lead from a student who, on speech day, wore a tee shirt emblazoned with FCUK, the irreverent French Connection United Kingdom clothing logo. His curious audience got sidetracked unscrambling the letters. Another classroom gem? The laid-back guy who wore a Budweiser tee shirt while arguing for stricter drunk-driving penalties. On a more delicate fashion theme, a speech isn't the best time to showcase a revealing outfit. Save the plunging V-neck tank top for a less formal occasion. Provocative apparel may draw attention away from your presentation, and blatant ogling can unsettle both speaker and observant audience members alike. Don't let your clothing undermine your message. If you dress like you have something important to say, audience members will listen for something of importance.

Finally, nothing gets a speaker even more nervous than appearing rattled in front of a crowd. Clothing can solve two common problems: blushing and leg tremors. Regarding the first item, women's skin is thinner and more translucent than men's, so women often blush more visibly than men. If you are a fair-skinned woman with a tendency to blush, consider wearing a turtleneck, mock turtleneck, or modest blouse; as insurance, top it off with a sweater or business jacket. For both light-skinned men and women, avoid neutral colors like white or beige that make red pop out. You don't want to look like a talking fire hydrant.

Regarding the second item, a speaker's legs will sometimes shake a bit from adrenaline. For women, a pantsuit or relaxed jeans should conceal this; for men, loose-fitting pants or a pair of pleated business slacks can act as camouflage. Tensing and relaxing your leg muscles will also release this nervous energy without tipping off the audience.

One final bonus theme: Remember when you were a kid and the uniforms finally arrived for your youth sports team? Instant superstars! People elevate their behavior to match their attire — that's why nightclubs have dress codes. Wearing a special outfit for a talk just might bring your game up a level. And if your regal appearance commands the audience's attention, that's one less thing to worry about at the lectern. Having said that, don't wear brand-new clothes for a speaking engagement. Being the master of ceremonies is an awful time to discover the maddening itch of a fabric allergy or feel new shoes digging into your ankles. Finally, if that lucky penny or rabbit's foot stuffed into your purse or pocket ensures superhuman powers, why not bring it along?

Dressing strategically is just one more way to tilt the scales in your favor as a speaker. While you can argue that the plumage shouldn't make the bird's song more beautiful, some listeners find it difficult to separate the feathers from the warbler in mid-song. Multiple studies reveal that appearance affects jury decisions, mate selection, the hiring process, teacher behavior towards students, and even parents' behavior towards their own children. Public speakers don't get a free pass. As Roman poet Juvenal wrote nearly two thousand years ago, "Seldom do people discern eloquence under a threadbare cloak." While you don't need a $5 million Neiman Marcus credit line like Victoria Beckham, savvy clothing choices can help you relax while speaking. In the end, looking your best just might bring out your best.

44

Ignore This Second-Rate Advice

As I sat in the back of the classroom grading, eyeing my clipboard and stopwatch, the young woman at the front of the room chuckled during much of her speech. Her topic wasn't funny, so I became concerned. Was she using drugs? Alcohol? Perhaps hallucinating? We spoke privately after class and the student confessed that she had imagined everyone in the room naked during her speech. This quirky mental image had triggered her nervous laughter.

This silly piece of bare-bones advice is frequently given to nervous speakers. At a time when we desperately need our wits about us to read an audience, skillfully select words and ideas, and achieve our speaking purpose, mentally undressing an audience should be our last priority. "Thought precedes action," as philosophers have noted for centuries. Disengaging the mind from what's coming out of the mouth is a bad idea, as this red-faced young woman learned.

Circus tycoon P. T. Barnum famously observed, "There's a sucker born every minute." The world is full of hucksters offering snake-oil solutions to complex problems, and it's no surprise that a colorful shelf of potions beckons to those who suffer from speech anxiety. Let's yank out the stoppers and pour a few more bottles of ersatz elixir down the drain.

Looking over people's heads is a second well-intended piece of advice worth ignoring. Variations encourage a speaker to focus on the ears or foreheads of audience members. If you were conversing with someone who stared at your ear, how would you feel about that person? Would you make a mental note of the nearest exit? "If I don't look at the audience, I won't see any negative reactions," is the thinking. But if you don't look at the audience, there *will* be negative reactions. Think of it this way: Giving a talk is like holding a conversation with a large group of people. Looking someone in the eye creates a bond and also provides valuable feedback while you speak. You risk losing both your speaking compass and the audience's goodwill by checking out people's hairlines as you present.

A third piece of wayward advice encourages a speaker to write out his or her entire talk. As a result, many speakers cling needlessly to anything they can type or scribble words on — index cards, loose-leaf paper, presentation slides. Nothing sounds duller than the singsong droning of a speaker with no theatrical training, particularly when the text being read also appears on slides or handouts. If the audience has cue cards, what's the point of having a speaker? Here's another perspective. If a friend called and wanted some pointers about golf — knowing that you had prepared a presentation on the topic — would you say, "Hang on! Let me grab my notes, turn on my computer, and fire up my Power Point slides"? No, you'd happily share the information. Natural memory, aided by a key-word outline, is the speaker's best ally.

A fourth dicey strategy advises speakers to warm up the audience with a joke. Once you get a crowd laughing, so the logic goes, everything will proceed smoothly. Jokes, however, carry a great risk of offending others. Just beyond your listeners' standard-issue blue jeans, coffee cups, and iPads buzzes a hornets' nest of religious, political, sexual, ethnic, cultural, and gender differences. During an informative speech, for example, one of my edgier students jested that Leonardo da Vinci's Mona Lisa was an "ugly chick." Nearly every female in class, many of Italian descent, squinted at him through brown eyes framed by cascades of brown shoulder-length hair. Thud. If you like to joke, joke about yourself; it's a much safer bet.

Let's quickly deep-six a few more popular public speaking no-nos. Ingesting distilled spirits to "take the edge off" is a foolish risk. Alcohol is a depressant that in sufficient amounts will make you slur words, weep, blurt out silly things, and smell like a brewery. Although you may feel relaxed, these side effects will not advance your career, reputation, or speaking purpose.

Speaking of drink, avoid guzzling coffee or other caffeinated beverages just before a presentation. Your sympathetic nervous system will squirt glucose and adrenaline into your bloodstream anyway, so you don't need another stimulant. Caffeine shifts many tongues into overdrive, and nervous speakers tend to talk fast as it is. When handling notes or visual aids after a double-double mocha grande, your hands might also shake like a greenhorn gunslinger in a B-rated western—not exactly the picture of confidence.

In summary, if hiking into the Grand Canyon, I'd much rather have a trail guide who is sober, keeping his eye on the path ahead, not relying on cue cards, not making blonde jokes, and definitely not thinking about me naked. For all the other bogus stage fright cures that I haven't heard about and those the human mind has yet to invent, the antidote is the same: Don't do anything that interferes with making a genuine connection with your audience. Remember, you are the bridge that joins listeners to your material. Most gimmicks are attempts to run away on the inside while standing in place on the outside. You will never succeed with your feet on the floor and your head out the door.

Our take-away message today: Managing speech anxiety is as much about what *not* to do as what *to* do. Using trickery to manipulate the speaking situation just won't work. Do things the old-fashioned way—stand your ground, speak from the heart, and keep things real.

45

Turn the Tables, If Needed

SOME AUDIENCES WILL TEST SPEAKERS. ON THE VERY RARE occasion when an unruly crowd threatens to get out of hand, you must turn the tables. Here's an example. Some years ago I heard Ed Koch, former mayor of New York City, speak at Princeton University. Not long into his talk, a group of hecklers shouted him down from the rafters. The feisty former mayor, lawyer, and congressman barked an order to turn on the house-lights, directed the theater's spotlights at the offenders, and then challenged them to shout out their protests. The mortified loud-mouths sat in silence. Koch retorted, "You really don't have much to say, do you? That's what I thought." The crowd cheered, and the hecklers slinked out when the houselights dimmed.

This anecdote illustrates two key points. First, you're in charge as the speaker — not the audience. Speakers sometimes mistakenly feel as if they're at the mercy of a throng, waiting for a cascade of frowns, folded arms, and bored yawns to dampen their courage. This is a flawed point of view. You decide what gets said, who gets paid attention to, and how and when listeners can speak. You also get to stand up and walk around; spectators typically remain seated in their chairs. You can talk and gesture freely; audience members must listen and restrain their movements. The word on the street? You're the kingpin of the playground.

Moving on to our second point, Mayor Koch demonstrated the basic principle behind turning the tables—violate a norm. Who would expect a speaker to blanket lecture-goers with spotlights? When you don't abide by all the conventions of public address, audiences don't know what you'll do next, and they will be less likely to violate a norm. To wit, listeners will behave better and pay more attention, thus surrendering control of the speaking venue to you. That's how turning the tables works.

Feeling a bit highbrow at first, I did *not* want to include this chapter in the book. Then I realized how often educators use this strategy. Think back to the classroom maneuvers of your grammar school teachers: laser-beam stares that could melt brains; long, stony silences that crushed sidebar chatter; baffling questions that would stump Einstein if a pupil dozed off. Teachers know that audiences are not always collections of angels. I worked as a substitute teacher in junior high schools for a time, so I know. In this role, you learn one lesson quickly—if you don't have control of the group, they have control of you. And if you don't feel in charge as the speaker, your anxiety level will soar past the rafters. In fact, novice teachers who leave the profession often cite unruly classrooms as a factor in their decision. For your own sake and that of civil audience members, you need to jerk in the reins when the horses run wild. Foul times call for foul deeds.

When you have a case of the jitters, though, communicating power with your body and voice can be difficult. My advice? Just strike a pose and play the role. Pull a prop from your bag of tricks and start improvising: Strut down the auditorium aisles. Bellow out key points. Gesture boldly. Call on people out of the blue. Push a chair aside. Do accents from *The Sopranos.* Channel a drill sergeant. Toss your jacket across a chair. Hike up your sleeves. Hover over people who talk out of turn. Rest your foot against a desk. Cast an evil eye. Smack the wall to make a point. Raise your fist. Hold someone's gaze too long. Almost let out a cuss word. Stand your ground and take command of the space. And don't let anybody see you sweat. Sometimes you have to fake it until you make it.

Turning the tables is Crowd Control 101, a survival skill for speakers. Rather than fearing the audience, let them fear you. Rather than feeling intimidated, intimidate them. It's a white-collar version of the time-tested gridiron strategy: "The best defense is a good offense." Although certainly not suited for all temperaments or situations, it offers up some prime advantages. If saddled with a lot of nervous energy, you can put that high voltage to good use and keep the crowd amused, rein in an ornery group, appear less nervous while speaking, and feel emboldened by your own antics. Not bad for an otherwise white-knuckle day at the office.

A word of warning: Don't turn the tables over on your own foot. Banging your shoe on a table, as Soviet premier Nikita Khrushchev famously did during a 1960 United Nations General Assembly meeting, is way over the top. Violate norms in a prudent manner. If you offend group members—particularly your boss, teacher, or customers—turning the tables can backfire. Take your lead from Mayor Koch: Only break the glass in case of a true emergency.

With this caveat in mind, remember that you're supposed to be in charge as the speaker. By convention, you have been given control of the group. Human beings are herd animals and will follow someone's lead. If you are at the front of the room, you should hold the reins and set the pace. Turning the tables can help when it seems like a few rude spectators or your own fears might overwhelm you. So get those arms flailing and just fuhgeddaboutit. Sometimes ya gotta do whatcha gotta do.

46

"Damn the Torpedoes, Full Speed Ahead!"

AT THE BATTLE OF MOBILE BAY IN THE U.S. CIVIL WAR, Union admiral David Farragut ordered his small fleet of ships to sail past lethal floating mines with the now-famous order, "Damn the torpedoes, full speed ahead!" Presenting controversial ideas, often in the hope of persuading a group, can also feel like a headlong charge into oblivion. Whether a business meeting, city council hearing, courtroom appearance, classroom presentation, sales pitch, or protest rally, such tense occasions often heighten a speaker's sense of fear. Here are three calming pieces of wisdom for these pulse-quickening times.

First, remember that an audience doesn't have to agree with you for you to be right. The *ad populum*, or bandwagon, fallacy argues that truth lies in numbers; that is, the larger the crowd of people that does or believes something, the more likely it is to be true. Just a few hundred years ago, however, most everyone on the planet believed that it was flat and that the sun revolved around the earth. Truth easily eludes popular grasp. Consider Italian astronomer Galileo Galilei. When he deduced, through scientific observations, that the earth revolves around the sun, the Catholic Church convicted Galileo of heresy, forced him to recant his beliefs, and subjected the aging scientist to house arrest for the final nine years of his life. In the storied history of science, Galileo now looms giant-like. Perhaps Mahatma Gandhi summed it up best: "Even if you are a minority of one, the truth is the truth."

Next, if your ideas suffer the sting of rejection, know that you are in good company, historically. Socrates, Lech Walesa, Albert Schweitzer, Aleksandr Solzhenitsyn, Gandhi, scores of suffragettes, César Chávez, and Nelson Mandela all spent time in jail because of their views. Those on the leading edge may seem over the edge to those at the rear of the column. With hindsight being 20/20, however, yesterday's radical notions are today's hallowed norms. One generation's revolutionaries are the next's mainstream heroes. After long, bloody struggles against unjust status quos, Gandhi negotiated with British authorities to free India, Dr. Martin Luther King Jr. witnessed the passage of the Civil Rights Act of 1964, and Nelson Mandela served as the first black president of apartheid-free South Africa. Even the recalcitrant Roman Catholic Church pardoned Galileo in 1992, three hundred and fifty years after his death. As American politician Adlai Stevenson once observed, "All progress has resulted from people who took unpopular positions."

Finally, history reveals that the ideas of individuals are a potent antidote to groupthink and move organizations, nations, and the world forward. Since 1901, the Royal Swedish Academy of Sciences has awarded Nobel Prizes in chemistry, literature, medicine, peace, physics, and, beginning in 1969, economics. Past Nobel laureates include Marie Curie, Albert Einstein, Mother Teresa, and Martin Luther King Jr. Although small groups occasionally win the award, perusing over one hundred years of Nobel Prize recipients confirms that individuals most often capture this honor. To put it another way, a public speaking audience has never won the Nobel Prize, but audiences have been addressed by many Nobel Prize winners. Individuals, not groups, move along the cutting edge.

Returning to our Civil War battle, Admiral Farragut's fleet struck many floating mines, but his risk paid off. Because of rusted triggers, Confederate mines harmlessly bounced off his ships' hulls and the Union Navy won the Battle of Mobile Bay. Hopefully, any mines strewn along your path will likewise be duds, and the audience will accept your message. If not, muster the minesweeping insights above into service as part of your public speaking battle plan.

VI

Stepping Down and
Looking Back

47

Give Yourself Approval

FROM THE MOMENT OF BIRTH WE ARE JUDGED. SECONDS after our arrival, medical personnel check our heart rate, breathing, muscle tone, skin color, and reflexes, assigning a score from zero to ten on something called the Apgar scale. Judgment never ceases during life. A brief sampling of formal evaluations includes report cards, IQ tests, aptitude tests, placement tests, driving tests, and employee performance appraisals.

Public speaking subjects us to further public scrutiny. How you look, sound, move, speak, and think all go under the microscope. No wonder so many people retreat from giving presentations. It's like being evaluated by a beauty judge, vocal trainer, drama coach, English teacher, and speech professor all at the same time. The delicate petals of the rose are pulled off and inspected, one by one.

If we didn't care about the opinions of others, however, we wouldn't fear public speaking. But what are we afraid of? People who would themselves make mistakes noticing that we've made a mistake? People who would themselves feel nervous noticing that we seem nervous? Why give a group of flawed, mortal human beings called an "audience" the power to turn your guts into jello?

Danger lurks when we surrender the power of approval to others. World-class vocalist Barbra Streisand has won eight Grammy Awards, two Academy Awards, five Emmys, a Tony Award, and ten Golden Globes; she has recorded fifty-one gold albums and has a star on Hollywood's Walk of Fame. Yet for a period of twenty-seven years, from 1967 to 1994, Ms. Streisand didn't sing in public. In 1967, during a performance in New York's Central Park, she forgot the lyrics to three songs. Humiliated, this stellar entertainer retreated from the public eye for the better part of three decades. Psychologist Nathaniel Branden summed up her predicament in *The Power of Self-Esteem*: "Of all the judgments we pass in life, none is more important than the judgment we pass on ourselves." While worshipped by millions of fans the world over, Streisand's own harsh verdict imprisoned her for nearly thirty years, a stretch of time longer than most felons serve for murder.

Self-limiting fates befall the famous and anonymous alike. In my public speaking classes, students write self-evaluations after each presentation. I ask them to identify and comment on their strengths and shortcomings as fledgling speakers. It breaks my heart when students believe they did nothing well, even after receiving praise from me and their classmates and reviewing a digital recording of their performance. The censure of parents, teachers, and peers has apparently been so fully internalized that affirming themselves would seem like an exercise in poor judgment. When we exaggerate minor flaws, however, the mind becomes a cruel fun-house mirror that distorts our worth, talents, and prospects in life.

At moments like these, I remind students of a warning once posted in a British classroom: "The teacher could be wrong. Think for yourselves." Even educators—those charged with the quickening of intelligence—do not always recognize the stirrings of genius. Consider the following pupil evaluations from former grammar school teachers: Abraham Lincoln was called a daydreamer who asked foolish questions. Albert Einstein's teacher told him he would never amount to much. Amelia Earhart was on the wrong track with her interest in daredevil projects unfit for a young lady. Woodrow Wilson's parents were warned not to set their sights too high for him. And because he was so slow, schooling was deemed useless for seven-year-old Thomas Alva Edison.

Experts, let alone a hodgepodge crowd of amateurs called an audience, have long histories of mistaken opinions. Learning to give ourselves approval is therefore a critical task for speakers. Consider these reasons: If you search for acceptance outside of yourself, it may never come. Second, even if it does come—like the cascade of honors showered on Barbra Streisand—without a grounding in self-approval we may dismiss the praise of others as off target. Finally, you, not others, stand in the best place to evaluate yourself.

All the world knows you from the outside looking in; only you know yourself from the inside looking out. Only you know the effort it takes to speak. Maybe you were a success because you didn't read word-for-word from your notes. Maybe you were a success because you made the time limit. Maybe you succeeded because you finally felt comfortable enough to gesture. Only you know the peaks and valleys of your speaking journey. That being the case, it makes sense to create standards that ring true for you, claim the right to judge the worth of your own efforts, and let go of what others think.

When poachers capture wild monkeys in Africa, they camp around the monkeys until the troop relaxes in their presence.

In time, the poachers offer the monkeys bananas, inching closer and closer during each feeding. The emboldened monkeys eventually grab bananas right out of the poachers' hands. Do the trappers then whip out a net, billy club, or shackles? No, they simply don't let go of the banana. Rather than scamper off, the incensed monkeys get into a tug-of-war over the banana, and their captors walk them into a cage and lock the door behind them. The monkeys keep the bananas but lose their freedom. The moral of the story? Let go of the banana! When you can let go of the hunger for audience approval, the opinions of the crowd will no longer imprison you, and the cell door swings open. Keep the keys to success in your own hands. Give yourself the gift of approval.

48

Gaze into the Magic Mirrors

Your heart has stopped racing. Your palms have dried. Your mind is clear. The speech is over. Time now to review your performance.

When speakers ask, "Magic mirror on the wall, who is the fairest one of all?" they can gaze at their reflections in three different mirrors: audience feedback, their own memories, and video recordings. For reasons that we will soon explore, I hope that you rely on the latter.

Whatever your delusions of grandeur or disaster, videos don't lie. If you said "um" fifty-three times, you'll hear it, but if you did a brilliant job, you'll recognize that, too. Being filmed is a bit scary. I recall the first time that I recorded myself while teaching. When reviewing the tape I thought, "That's funny, all the students look and sound like they usually do, but I don't!" Smile, you're on *Candid Camera*. Whether it's a stodgy VHS model or the latest smartphone, that unblinking lens bears silent and unbiased witness to your strengths and weaknesses as a speaker.

Despite the numerous advantages, a few words of caution about video recordings are in order. First, two-dimensional camera images do not fully capture crowd feedback, speaker adjustments to these signals, or the rapport between presenter and audience. Although videos faithfully frame the biomechanics of speaking, the complex magic of the moment sometimes evaporates on tape. Blockbuster films typically cost a few hundred million to make for good reason: It's not easy to capture the nuances of life on film. But this is good news because, in all likelihood, you did even better than what appears on tape. In that regard, while they begrudgingly watch their videos, the vast majority of my students are pleasantly surprised by the results.

While on the topic of videos, be forewarned about the soundtrack: Many speakers do not like the sound of their own voices. Even superstar actress Angelina Jolie commented, "You know, when you hear your own voice, you can find it quite boring and uninteresting." Like a ticking clock placed on a wooden table, a speaker hears his or her own voice through both sound waves and bone conduction, so we sound a bit deeper and fuller to ourselves than we do to others. The crowd and camera, on the other hand, hear the thinner airborne pulse of sound waves only.

While lamenting the *sound* of the voice, many speakers might actually be unhappy with how they have *used* the voice. Like amateurs tinkering with the black keys of a piano, many presenters do not take full advantage of the rich timbre and broad expressive range of their vocal instruments. Try this simple technique to combat a dull-sounding voice: Raise the pitch and raise the volume of key words and ideas during your talk. Often called "telegraphing," this easy strategy is stock in trade for professional newscasters and sportscasters the world over. Boxing announcer Michael Buffer, for example, employs this technique during his trademarked "Let's get ready to rumble!"

Don't underestimate the power of telegraphing: According to ABC News, this well-delivered five-word line has earned Buffer over $400 million to date.

Whether or not you filmed your presentation, rely next on audience feedback. Like Rudyard Kipling's story of six blind men describing an elephant after each had touched a different part of its body, the location of audience members will color their perceptions. Survey people from different parts of the room for a balanced critique. You might seem too loud to someone sitting in the front row but too soft to someone listening in the back. The expertise of listeners will also affect their judgments, so guide audience members by soliciting feedback on specific areas of content and delivery most relevant to you. If enrolled in a speech class, you'll probably have standard evaluation sheets at your disposal for this purpose. If not, create your own. Lastly, when fielding comments about your presentation, remember that a listener's perception is his or her reality. Whether an audience member grabbed the elephant's trunk, tail, or leg, that subjective experience is all your listener knows. Learn from the unique images in each looking glass.

Your final source of feedback is your own memories. After critiquing thousands of self-assessments from classroom speakers, however, I've learned that a speaker's hindsight is rarely 20/20 but often riddled with blind spots, skewed perspectives, and fragmented recollections. Human memory is a recreation rather than a recording of the past. Anxious presenters will have difficulty recalling their own words, let alone judging their effectiveness as speakers. To encourage objectivity, trace back your performance along the stable girders of traditional speech structure. (See Chapter 32, "Snap the Pieces into Place," as a guide.) Inspect each element in the introduction, body, and conclusion, and then assess your verbal and nonverbal delivery skills. Keep in mind that the audience's view from the outside looking in is apt to be kinder than your view from the inside looking out.

In summary, rely first on the camera, next on the crowd, and lastly on yourself for feedback about a presentation. How does reviewing your performance relate to confident speaking? The equation is simple: the better your speaking performances, the less anxious you will feel. However, you won't know how well you've done until you peer into a mirror. After having the courage to speak, please muster up the courage to evaluate yourself. Push that Evil Queen aside and find your fairest self in Snow White's Magic Mirror.

49

See the Tree, Not the Leaves

WHEN A PERSON CAN'T SEE THE FOREST FOR THE TREES, he or she has become so lost in details that the big picture looms like a fog-shrouded blur. When students analyze their recorded speeches, this is the most common blunder that I observe.

"Did you notice that one of my ears is a bit lower than the other?"

"My voice sounded like Mickey Mouse when I began."

"What's wrong with me? My eyebrows twitched at the end of the speech."

The number and variety of self-castigating comments that I hear is dizzying, but they spring from a single, common root: a morbid obsession with minor flaws.

When students brood over petty performance blemishes, I ask them to imagine a tree in autumn. "The tree looks beautiful, no?" I will ask, but the decay and death of its leaves generate the many hues of the tree. And from a distance, a tree rarely appears symmetrical—it is often lopsided. And lovers have sometimes carved their initials in the bark, bark that may be riddled with insect holes. Nonetheless, every fall, tourists drive hundreds of miles to watch trees turn colors. Why be so impressed with all that imperfection? In brief — the whole of it, the grand vista, the sum beyond all of the parts, is beautiful.

In similar fashion, it's wise for speakers to step back and form a panoramic impression of a speech. Ask yourself what you did well in all areas — topic choice, content selection, structure, and physical and vocal delivery. While there will always be skinned knees and bruised elbows after your first few bicycle rides, take the time to notice, celebrate, and build on your strengths. Even with beginning speakers in an entry-level course, strengths typically outnumber weaknesses. Moreover, even if you wobble wildly as you ride across the finish line, consider that flaws add authenticity to human efforts. Nervousness betrays the importance of the topic to a speaker; unvarnished regional accents infuse a tale with local color; deep currents of emotion swirling through passages reveal humanity. While cool mechanistic perfection is an asset for expensive Swiss watches, many audiences will warmly embrace faltering yet sincere speakers.

Remember, too, that a speech is more than a sterile assembly of mechanical presentation parts. Intangibles factor into the calculus of speaking. Take, for example, a recent student of mine who served two combat tours of duty in Iraq. This young soldier and father had spent six years on the streets of Baghdad, Ramadi, and Mosul. Fit, ramrod straight, polite, and sober in his remarks, he looked and acted like a soldier. When he rose to speak, somewhat anxiously, about his firsthand experience of post-traumatic stress disorder (PTSD), the room fell silent. The mere presence of a speaker can project power. Back in the late 1800s, large crowds gathered to hear stately Chief Joseph of the Nez Percé address the plight of Native Americans — even though he couldn't speak English. Without saying a word, your dignity, demeanor, and quiet authority will impact and help you connect with an audience. Who you *are* — not just what you *say* — will help to win the day.

Keep in mind, also, that presenting is not a beauty pageant or vocal contest. While stellar looks, flawless articulation, and a sonorous voice might briefly entrance an audience, consider this: no sounds remain from some of the most famous speakers in history — Cicero, Socrates, Demosthenes, not even Abraham Lincoln. Only their words and ideas remain. But that is the whole point of speaking — it's not about how you look or how you sound but the *message* that you share. Prime minister Winston Churchill, for instance, exhorted the British Empire to rise up against the crushing forces of Nazi Germany in radio addresses that clearly broadcast his unmistakable lisp. King George VI, portrayed in the Oscar-winning film *The King's Speech*, suffered from a horrible stammer, yet pushed aside extreme self-consciousness to rally his subjects for the same noble war effort. Although Hitler was perhaps the better orator, the truths expressed by Churchill and King George prevailed and still echo in human consciousness.

When Zen Buddhist potters craft tea bowls, some intentionally chip the bottom of each cup to symbolize the lack of perfection in the universe. Like a tree turning colors in autumn, you, too, are part of the vibrant yet imperfect beauty of the natural world. Whether this is your first or fiftieth season as a speaker, learn to appreciate the whole rather than picking apart the minutiae of your performance. Obsessing about a stray lock of hair or mispronounced word will never do justice to the totality of your being or your audience.

50

Do Your Best and Let It Go

AUDIENCES, LIKE PEOPLE, HAVE THEIR OWN PERSONALITIES. As a community college professor teaching a large general education course, I sometimes teach five sections of the same public speaking course during a term. Seeing each class react is fascinating. One group will love a topic or exercise; another will respond coolly. One section will love my jokes; another will roll their eyes. I can be a genius in the eight o'clock class and a dunce in the two o'clock class. A few weeks later, the pattern might reverse itself.

Watching groups respond differently to the same material has taught me an important lesson. As hard as I work to get things right, audience reactions are ultimately out of my hands. This makes teaching easier. As a professional, I gather and present the best lessons, exercises, and assignments that I can muster up and then let go of the results. I can only control my end of the educational bargain. How any audience reacts is a function of its unique chemistry and personality along with fickle variables like the weather and time of day. As any stand-up comic knows, they can love you in Vegas and hate you in Reno.

Accepting this fact is hard for some speakers. Showoffs want to wow everyone. But if you are a parent, in a romantic relationship, or dealing with the troubling habits of a loved one, you know how difficult it is to control another's behavior. Read the word "difficult" here as "impossible." If we can't control the behavior of a squirmy little three-year-old kid—or her pet cat—how can we hope to control the perceptions and reactions of an audience comprised of dozens, hundreds, or even thousands of diverse adults?

Since I teach so many sections of the same class, however, you might think that I would quickly learn what works and what doesn't work with my audiences. But teaching, like public speaking, is not an exact science. Cultures constantly change, along with the collections of individuals they produce called audiences. What works in one time and place doesn't work in another time and place. What works with the choir might leave the congregation cold. Learning by trial and error never ends. Although most of my classes and students respond positively, that doesn't always happen. After engaging thousands of students in the classroom, I know that many believe my course has changed their lives for the better while others might believe that I'm the biggest oaf who ever laced up a pair of Oxfords and roamed the earth. I don't get everything right every time. Who does?

Given that public speaking is hard enough, you don't want to climb aboard the everybody-will-just-love-my-perfect-speech roller coaster with your gut already churning. Here's the stomach-soothing tonic: While remaining sensitive to the needs of the audience, learn to become even-keeled about their responses. If I took every frown, eye roll, and jab at public speaking to heart, I would never again set foot in a classroom. Likewise, if I took every smile, peal of laughter, and word of praise to heart, my head wouldn't fit through the lecture-hall door. With this sobering perspective in mind, the calculus of public speaking becomes simple: Set a goal, and then set out to achieve that goal. On the day that you speak, as the person you are, with the skills, knowledge, and aptitudes you possess, do the best you can and let it go. In the long run, the only winning formula is to measure success not by how the audience *reacts* but by how you have chosen to *act*.

When working on their speeches, students sometimes ask for guidance about the use of quotations. I tell them, if a credible source said it better than you, use the quote and give the author credit. I'll follow my own advice by closing with a passage from President Abraham Lincoln:

> If I care to listen to every criticism, let alone act on them, then this shop may as well be closed for all other businesses. I have learned to do my best, and if the end result is good then I do not care for any criticism, but if the end result is not good, then even the praise of ten angels would not make the difference.[1]

Who can argue with that?

VII

The Big Picture

51

You Just Might Change
the World

ALL DAY LONG, EVERY DAY OF THE YEAR, COSMIC RAYS
stream in from outer space at nearly 186,000 miles per
second. These powerful yet invisible energy streams bathe the
earth and every life form on it, randomly mutating the DNA of
unsuspecting creatures. Like these imperceptible rays, your ideas
can also trigger an alteration, but in someone's thinking—a mu-
tation of the mind. Since beliefs drive our behavior as much as
DNA, new viewpoints *do* have the power to make anyone walk
away a changed person.

While no one can put a finger on the planet and make it
spin in a different direction, speakers have long been catalysts
for lasting change. World history provides some clear examples. In nineteenth-century England, William Wilberforce's
oratory helped bring about an end to the colonial slave trade;
Katherine Sheppard's advocacy made New Zealand the first
nation to grant women the right to vote; Gandhi's campaign
of noncooperation freed 300 million in India from oppressive
British rule; President Woodrow Wilson's vision inspired the

birth of the United Nations; and Dr. Martin Luther King Jr. derailed institutionalized racism in America.

While the scattershot spray of cosmic rays randomly mutates species, the conscious introduction of ideas into society purposefully alters human thinking and behavior. This perspective offers a liberating slant on speech anxiety. What if you could change the world when you spoke? Wouldn't you feel great confidence? Wouldn't your fears shrink in size, knowing the tremendous impact you might have?

You can argue, of course, that you don't speak on a world stage, but you do speak on a stage in someone's world. In my speech classes, for example, students walk away knowing about medical advances, key events and figures from history, finances, self-defense tactics, and first-aid procedures. They also reconsider their views on gun control, climate change, the death penalty, drug and alcohol use, and scores of other vital issues. Their worlds *are* changed by the words spoken in them.

Taking a broader view, your audience is not limited to those sitting before you. The play *Six Degrees of Separation*, written by John Guare, hints at the short chain of human connections that links us to others. Although the play is based on a short story by Hungarian writer Frigyes Karinthy, research by psychologist Stanley Milgram and recent studies by Facebook and Twitter have found that we are, in fact, removed from anyone in the world by around five people.[1] Ideas shared in public, then, are just a few private exchanges away from any king, queen, president, or prime minister on earth.

Whatever the promises of the human grapevine, at first glance changing the world seems preposterous. Yet we notice that the world changes anyway and that human beings are responsible. Take the case of Jean-Henri Dunant. In 1859, this Swiss businessman witnessed the agony and death of

40,000 soldiers who were wounded during the Battle of Solferino in Italy. After fighting bravely, casualties were left behind on battlefields to be shot, looted, bayoneted, trampled by horses, crushed by cannon, and swarmed by flies and maggots. No medic or ambulance corps came to the rescue. Unless soldiers rose under their own power, their part in the glories of war had ended.

Appalled by their unaided suffering, Dunant wrote an eyewitness account of the battle called *A Memory of Solferino*, published the book at his own expense, distributed it to the royal courts of Europe, and met with four influential friends who brainstormed ways to end the neglect of fallen soldiers. Dunant's concerns soon echoed in government halls and military quarters throughout Europe. A well-attended international congress organized by Dunant's small group of friends took place in Switzerland.

As a result of this conference, a dozen powerful nations agreed for the first time in history that wounded soldiers, regardless of nationality, should be systematically collected and cared for during battle. Since the meeting was held in Geneva, the ten articles ratified by government delegates were called the Geneva Convention. With this agreement as its birthmark, the Red Cross was born in 1864. Now 100 million members strong, volunteers of the International Federation of Red Cross and Red Crescent Societies aid the victims of natural and manmade catastrophes the world over.[2] Millions of soldiers, disaster victims, and their descendants owe their lives to Jean-Henri Dunant, one person who spoke up about a practice that is now universally condemned.

In a book quite different from Dunant's lament on war, a once-obscure German leader wrote, "The power which set sliding the greatest historical avalanches of political and religious nature was, from the beginning of time, the magic force of the spoken word alone." Adolf Hitler tested his theory with brutal results. As world leaders throughout history have shown, public speaking does sway public opinion. Be mindful of its power. Whether touching listeners in the room or influencing events a thousand miles away, whenever you stand and speak some part of the world will change, for better or worse.

52

Dedicate Your Speech

THE IRONMAN TRIATHLON ON THE KONA COAST OF HAWAII
is one of the most grueling tests of human endurance.
Athletes swim 2.4 miles in open seas, bicycle 112 miles, and *then*
run a 26.2-mile marathon—all without taking a break. Elite
world record holders need over eight hours to complete the
event; mere mortals must finish within seventeen hours. According to a USA Triathlon study, 38 deaths occurred in sanctioned
events between 2006 and 2011 alone.[3]

Despite the dangers, retired lieutenant colonel Dick Hoyt
completed an Ironman Triathlon in Kona at the age of sixty-
five—pretty impressive for a senior citizen. Through 2012,
however, Hoyt has finished over 1,050 other races, including
five additional Ironmans, nearly 250 triathlons, and 70 mara-
thons. In 1992, he also ran and bicycled across America, a feat
that took 45 days and covered 3,735 miles. The hard part?
He pushed his son Rick in a wheelchair or pulled him along
in a special boat during each race. Hoyt's son is a quadriplegic
with cerebral palsy, and he wants his son—an integral of

"Team Hoyt"—to enjoy all areas of life. Their team slogan is "Yes You Can."

Dick Hoyt embodies a profound truth. When people dedicate their efforts to others, they often achieve far more than they ever dreamt possible. With another's welfare at stake we set the bar higher, hoe the row longer, and endure more suffering than we might for ourselves alone. Everyday examples abound. Firefighters rush into burning buildings to rescue total strangers. Soldiers risk all in combat to protect the life and liberty of distant countrymen. Immigrants arrive penniless on foreign soil, hoping their children will one day lead better lives. No other species exhibits this selfless behavior more often than humans. Perhaps we carry a gene for it.

The creative among us routinely dedicate songs, poems, plays, ships, bridges, buildings, and performances to others, so why not a speech? Four advantages come to mind. First, the energy needed to research and rehearse your presentation will bubble up from a deep wellspring. The more deserving your person, the greater your motivation. Second, the caliber of your effort will soar with someone worth honoring as its inspiration. You wouldn't want to let down your uncle suffering from stage IV cancer; he deserves better. Third, you will derive great emotional satisfaction from your presentation. You aren't just giving a speech; you're giving the best of your heart and mind as a special gift. Finally, you will hold the moral high ground while speaking. During the persuasive round of talks in speech class, students seeking blood donors, canned goods for needy families, or holiday gifts for combat troops usually muster up a stronger mojo than the pot-should-be-legal-now-so-I-can-get-stoned-in-the-parking-lot orator. This "gravitas" or emotional heft will beef up the speaking persona of even a timid advocate.

Applying this strategy is easy. First, call to mind a person or group worthy of your dedication. If the person is alive, tell him or her about your effort—issue an invitation to your talk if you like. If no longer on earth, honor this person's ongoing presence in your life in a way that makes sense to you. In either case, you must elevate your craftsmanship to its highest level, since your speech is a gift. Pay attention to every detail. Add verbal bows and ribbons to your handiwork.

If the honoree is not present during your speech, you can place a picture on the lectern as a memento. No one in the audience needs to know or see what you're doing, by the way. Unless giving a eulogy or wedding toast, avoid a dedication announcement that seems overly sentimental or out of place for the speaking occasion. A gift offered in the private chambers of your heart is no less a gift.

Whether your grandmother smiles down on you from the heavens or your spouse smiles from the balcony, dedicating your speech will help you overcome self-limiting fears and doubts. Rise to the occasion and honor someone special with the gift of a speech. Show them and the rest of the world that you can do what they always believed you could do: Stir the hearts and minds of listeners through the artful use of your words and voice.

53

Why Fear Ghosts?

THIS STRATEGY IS NOT FOR THE FAINT-OF-HEART. IF YOU feel squeamish about death, read no further. Okay, are all the kids out of the room? Then let's talk.

One of my favorite photographs is "Grand Central Station," taken in 1934 by Sir Edward Hulton. All the adults in this famous photograph, milling around in fedoras and overcoats, are presumably dead by now. Even a baby in the picture would today be roughly eighty years old. This god's-eye view of a busy railroad terminal reminds me of the fleeting nature of life. We are here for a few moments, cosmically speaking, moving to and from our appointed destinations before departing.

Nowhere is this limited sense of time more keen than on death row. After the years and months have dwindled down to minutes, prison guards lead the condemned to execution by yelling out, "Dead man walking." This practice became the title of a book by Sister Helen Prejean and a movie starring Oscar-winning actor Sean Penn. Although we enjoy greater freedom outside prison walls, we only differ from death-row inmates in that we do not yet know the hour of our death. We are all dead men walking.

Religion, philosophy, and other forms of spirituality grapple with this unkind shock of our human mortality. The Buddhist practice of cemetery meditations, for example, seeks to weaken both the fear of death and the hold our living brethren have over us. Intrigued by this practice as a junior in high school, I bicycled to a local graveyard one warm night, respectfully sat against an oak tree, and meditated under a blanket of vibrant summer stars. At first, I felt uneasy. Among many thousands of silent companions, I was the only one breathing. Then I relaxed. They had their journeys, I thought, now I have mine.

As indelicate as these thoughts may seem, reflecting on our mortality can empower speakers. How can these somber ruminations aid you? In all likelihood, any audience you fear will be lined up under a neat row of grave markers within one hundred years. Each human life, no matter how grand, resolves itself into dust, ashes, and memories. So when you stand before a crowd, imagine that each person has already left this mortal plane and passed on to other worlds. Will you allow a group of ghosts to keep you from speaking your mind? Will you let those who temporarily enjoy life in their limbs steal the breath out of yours?

Generations of human beings rise and fall like waves upon a vast sea, but the swell of life is still within you. This is your time. These are your moments. When facing an audience, stand tall, seize the chance, and speak your mind. The Latin expression for this sentiment is *carpe diem*, "Seize the day." If the village tongues wag, let them. It takes courage to speak *to* others, but it takes little courage to speak *about* others.

Legend tells us that Alexander the Great's hands dangled outside the coffin during his funeral procession. As a parting lesson, his subjects saw that the ruler of the entire known world had no power to stop death and left his kingdom empty-handed. Being alive, you are more powerful than a thousand dead kings. Choose your words with care when you speak. Keep in mind the brevity of life but the longevity of ideas. Generations after their original audiences have left the earth, the winds of voices still carry the seeds of worthwhile ideas around the world.

54

Speak as a Spiritual Act

AS A FIFTEEN-YEAR-OLD SITTING IN REQUIRED HIGH school Latin classes, the real-life value of studying a dead language eluded me. But every English word has a history, and that history often traces back to Latin or Greek. The words *inspire* and *spirit*, for example, share a common root: the Latin noun *spiritus*, which means breath, life, soul, or spirit. For many, a spiritual act is thus an inspired act, one often rooted—as author Maya Angelou suggests—in a power larger and other than ourselves.

Being mindful of the lessons of history and our human foibles, however, I offer the advice in this chapter with some caution. Not every human compass—personal or organizational—points to true north. Regardless, many have found it a potent antidote for speech anxiety, as those sharing inspired messages often feel girded by tremendous courage. Reverend Martin Luther King Jr., for example, was stabbed, jailed, spat upon, pelted with rocks, bowled over by fire hoses, rocked by bomb attacks at two homes, and tormented by countless death threats. Despite these hateful actions, on April 3, 1968, in Memphis, Tennessee, Dr. King proclaimed, "I'm not worried about anything. I'm not fearing any man." The next day he was assassinated. And therein lies the power of speaking as a spiritual act. What can intimidate a speaker who has no fear of death? What can stand in the way of an orator who feels called on by the divine? Not even the most virulent strain of speech anxiety will rein in such a voice.

Public speaking as a spiritual practice defies neat categorization and departs from other cut-and-dried techniques in this book. Whether on a small or grand scale, otherworldly inspiration does not fit neatly into a how-to format. Like genius or creativity, it can't be whittled down to a coarse rule of thumb. So, if you ask how, it may be best to follow the tug of your own heart and conscience. And if you ask why, know that a genuine calling may instead leave you asking when and where. To invoke the man-in-the-street defense, making these decisions for you is above my rank and pay grade. Who am I to decide what is religious or spiritual for every reader of this book?

If still curious about how to press on, here's a toehold for your spiritual ascent: Speech itself is a miracle. We are the only species out of millions that uses both oral and written language. Human beings communicate in over 6,000 tongues, and as members of the planet's premier message-making species, there is certainly room for the miraculous when we speak. Even Shakespeare weighed in on the metaphysical. While discussing the prospect of ghosts with his friend Horatio, Prince Hamlet observed, "There are more things in heaven and earth, Horatio, than are dreamt of in your philosophy." The truly inspired speaker steps into this larger realm where grand things are possible.

With the universal flame of intelligence as a guiding light, any of us can receive a genuine calling to share a sliver of the transcendent with our mortal brethren. Nineteenth-century writer Henry Van Dyke put it this way: "The woods would be very silent if no birds sang except those that sang best." Everyone has wisdom to share. Everyone has a story to tell. In this broader sense, a "vocation"—the receipt of a religious calling—extends beyond the walls of mosques, temples, churches, and synagogues and into the community-at-large. Even a solitary candle will cast light on a darkened path.

In this humble manner, we can embrace public speaking as a spiritual practice. Anyone can offer up a speech as a communal gift. Anyone can stand as a witness to a small or large truth. Anyone can gracefully surrender to a grander purpose, if only for a few moments. So, if the spirit calls and you feel inspired to speak from your heart-of-hearts, know that a ray of starlight might just slip through your being at the lectern, grounding you from afar with the strength and wisdom of the cosmos.

55

100 Years from Now,
Will It Matter?

VISIT ANY ART MUSEUM AND YOU WILL BE STRUCK BY HOW quickly human eras come and go. Visit any natural history museum and you will marvel at the rise and fall of geologic epochs. Astrophysicists estimate the age of the universe at about fourteen billion years, and life on earth has marched on for a few billion of those. Why then do we feel that the stars and planets will be yanked from their celestial moorings by a mishap during one of our speeches?

Although your heart may pound, palms sweat, and thoughts race when faced with a speech, putting things in the big picture will help you succeed in the small picture. Try these two simple experiments for a shift of perspective. First, look at a calendar. What is today's date? Now, think of three things that happened about a century ago. Okay, two. How about one? Nothing comes to mind? Don't you recall the sinking of the *Titanic* in 1912, Henry Ford introducing the moving assembly line in 1913, or the start of World War I in 1914? If not, take heart from your forgetfulness. Researchers in the next century will also draw a blank if asked about your presentation. Even if you faint and get whisked out on a stretcher—which will never happen, by the way—they won't find any stories in the *London Times*, *Washington Post*, or your local newspaper. As Roman emperor Marcus Aurelius observed some 1,900 years ago in his book *Meditations*, "In a little while, the memory of all things is swallowed up in eternity."[4]

Next, in your mind's eye, watch your presentation from a vantage point inside the room where it will occur. Now, watch from your state capital; then from your nation's capital; then the moon, the sun, the edge of our Milky Way galaxy; and now the farthest reaches of the universe. Can you still see yourself speaking from a billion light-years away? Probably not. A light-year, as you may know, is a measure of distance—5,865,696,000,000 miles. One small speech in one tiny corner of the universe just won't show up on any cosmic map.

Please don't misunderstand me. Effective public speaking does change lives in communities, nations, and the world. I teach communication courses because I believe in their value. Amidst the vastness of time and space, however, any speech will shrink in significance. Let this embolden you. Leave the reporters, photographers, speech critics, and historians at the door. The less momentous your talk seems, the more relaxed you will feel while delivering it, and the better you will do. And the more effective your presentation, the greater its impact, and the more moving and memorable it will be to an audience. Paradoxically, sensing the relative unimportance of any particular speech in the grand scheme frees you to do immeasurably better in the here and now.

Zen Buddhist masters give monks short riddles to solve called *koans*. Mull over this paradox of public speaking: In the big picture it doesn't seem to matter, but in the small picture it matters a lot. A drop in a pond gets swallowed up, but a drop in a puddle makes waves. Prepare like it matters, and then relax as if it doesn't matter. As Mahatma Gandhi said, "Whatever you do will be insignificant, but it is very important that you do it." When you can embrace these contradictory truths simultaneously, you hold a shining golden key to powerful public speaking in your hands.

56

Your Life Is a Speech

ON THE LAST DAY OF PUBLIC SPEAKING CLASS, IF THE weather and mood of the class permit, we venture outside for one final speech. After students finish their tribute speeches in the warmth and light of spring, I divulge a secret that I've kept from them the entire term: This class has prepared them for life.

Such a saccharine revelation would never be tolerated on any day except the last day of class, so I take advantage of their sleeping sentries and trumpet a parting message over unmanned battlements. "Life is like a speech," I tell them. "Life, in fact, is one long speech. Everything you need to know about life, you just learned in speech class."

Before their collective eyes begin to roll, I start a defense of the proposition. "There are sixteen ways that your life is like a speech," I proclaim. "The tasks of living and public speaking stand shoulder-to-shoulder on common ground." Let me now share this parting perspective with you as our time together draws to a close:

1) Each task—whether ventured for eight minutes or eighty years—involves finding your own voice, your own truth, and expressing yourself.

2) We learn the ins and outs of both living and public speaking by doing. Progress and mastery do not come while sitting on the sidelines.

3) Public speaking is a risk, like life itself. Playing it safe yields few rewards.

4) Fears arise because worthwhile ends and ambitions are at stake. Only when our hearts aren't in it, do we not care about what we say or do.

5) Other people count. To succeed with audience members or your daily circle of connections, you must keep in mind the wants, needs, and interests of those around you.

6) Each endeavor is a chance to serve others. Communal service is, in fact, often the highest aim of public speaking and a sublime end of living.

7) Each undertaking has a beginning, middle, and end. How well you prepare for one stage will affect the outcome of the next.

8) Because planning and sound reasoning are required in both speeches and life, there is a need for logic, or *logos*, as the Greek philosopher Aristotle taught.

9) Planning should not stop you, however, from seizing unexpected opportunities. Spontaneity is important in both effective speaking and worthwhile living.

10) Honesty is the best policy. If you steal someone's ideas, you cheat yourself out of both learning and authenticity at the lectern. If you live someone else's dream, you cheat yourself out of a life.

11) On the podium and on your daily pathways, it's wise to speak up, stand your ground, and look people in the eye.

12) In both speaking and living, it's good to breathe, relax, and pace yourself.

13) No matter how well you prepare, you will always make mistakes. The common goal of public speaking and life, however, is progress, not perfection. To be effective, you need not be perfect.

14) The same universal breath forms words and sustains life. To be the creator of spoken words or a creature that draws in life-giving breath is a privilege.

15) Heartfelt passion is the true spice of both engaged living and engaging speaking.

16) And, finally, whether a good speech or a good life, you should never rush to reach the end. The journey is the goal, not your parting words.

This humble comparison sketches out my sometimes oversized enthusiasm for the course. I get excited about teaching public speaking because of its connection to the larger journey of life. If my profession was all about teaching students to stand still and avoid saying "um," I just couldn't do it. Fortunately, the art of speaking offers greater depth.

In truth, public speaking is a way of turning ourselves inside out and making our private selves known to the world. The fear of speaking is symbolic of the fear that we all face on the journey of knowing and becoming ourselves in a world that is not always loving or hospitable. At its deepest level, public speaking can help with your emergence as an individual, in both thought and deed. As poet Walt Whitman wrote in "O Me! O Life!," "The powerful play goes on, and you will contribute a verse."

On the last day of class, I tell students, "Although the class is over, your real speeches are just beginning." Likewise, although the book is over, your real speech is about to begin. The extent to which you feel fear while presenting may be the extent to which unowned parts of yourself lay waiting to be claimed. The extent to which you feel excitement while speaking may be the degree to which you've already seized upon vibrant parts of yourself. In brief, the courage to speak is the courage to embrace your own life and truths.

With that final lesson on the board, class is dismissed. Time now to stand and speak. Find your own voice, be heard, and make a difference. Please join the chorus. There is one voice missing.

I

OPENING VISTAS

SUMMARY

Fear of public speaking is commonplace. Politicians, entertainers, business professionals, and notables throughout history have felt its grip before and while presenting. Most speakers succeed, however, despite communication apprehension. These presenters learn that we often judge ourselves more harshly than our listeners, and they accept fear as an invitation to growth—both personal and professional. In fact, since many fear public speaking more than anything else, speaking in public can spur levels of growth unlike anything else. If you simply take the time before speaking to challenge old stereotypes about speaking, it will change your experience while presenting. Anyone can leave behind the fear of public speaking, if they wish.

Points to Ponder

1. Ask friends, relatives, classmates, and coworkers if they become nervous before giving a presentation. If so, how

do they calm themselves down? Can you apply any of their strategies?

2. Read through the list of notables who have experienced speech anxiety in Chapter 2. Research a person who interests you and see how he or she overcame nervousness. Can you apply their approach?

3. Generate a list of fears that you have overcome in the past. What steps did you take to outgrow each fear? Can you imagine a similar process and outcome with public speaking?

4. Imagine a world where no one had the courage to stand up and speak about problems or injustices. How would your life and the lives of those around you be different?

5. Can you think of a time when you erroneously believed that others noticed a mistake that you had made and you felt self-conscious? Do you think this might happen with audiences when you speak in public?

6. If you had all the courage in the world, what would you speak about? What small step can you take today towards fulfilling that dream?

II

BASIC STRATEGIES

SUMMARY

As you shift from thinking about a speech to actually preparing a speech, use the many cognitive and behavioral tools at your disposal. Realize that fear supplies us with energy during every step of the speechmaking process, if we're willing to embrace it. This energy can propel you to prepare mentally, physically, and emotionally before speaking in public. Remember, too, that a presentation is more like a conversation with an audience than a theatrical performance. Reaching out to friends and family members for support as you gather your ideas and practice your speech is a natural way to prepare for this "conversation." The more you plan for potential mistakes and practice in front of a live audience, the more confident you will feel at the lectern. A successful speech is not a matter of luck; it's a matter of preparation.

Points to Ponder

1. Reflect on the fears you have about speaking in public. Use the reframing strategy described in Chapter 7 to

discover "what could be good" about them. How might these fears energize rather than discourage you?

2. Review the six differences between a speech and a theatrical performance outlined in Chapter 8. Do you hold any of these limiting views of public address? If so, how can you change your perspective?

3. Think about an upcoming presentation that you will give. Map out the steps and timeline needed for your cognitive, physical, and emotional preparation.

4. Identify people in your circle of friends and family who might be sources of help for your speech preparation. While being careful to avoid plagiarism, what specific steps do you think each could help you with the most?

5. Hold a dress rehearsal for your speech with a practice audience. Immediately following your rehearsal, ask for feedback about the content and delivery of your talk. What did you learn? What comments were most helpful to you?

6. In Chapter 12, we learn that each talk is for a particular audience in a particular setting on a particular occasion. Think of a speech you have attended or viewed. How might the audience, setting, and occasion have influenced the speaker's choices in preparing for and presenting the speech? How might these variables influence your next presentation?

7. In addition to those listed in Chapter 13, identify three potential mishaps that might occur during your next talk. What backup plans could you develop for each?

8. What physical activities or types of exercise do you enjoy most? Which of these do you think would be most helpful to you in burning off nervous energy before a speech?

9. Think of a situation in which you enjoyed performing in front of a live audience. Why did you enjoy it? How might you be able to connect that enjoyment to public speaking?

10. Research other communication courses that your school or local training organizations offer. Which ones interest you the most? What benefits could you gain from them?

III

COGNITIVE STRATEGIES

SUMMARY

People have much more experience in public speaking than they realize. We "give speeches" every day while communicating with friends, classmates, and coworkers. Why is it then that so many of us struggle with anxiety at the podium? Whenever we reach for a goal, the desire for success and acceptance creates the fear of failure and rejection. When we transform misguided, limiting beliefs about public speaking into positive, supportive thoughts, however, we discover the benefits of moving beyond our fears. Be patient with yourself as you learn to manage your anxiety and discover your unique pathway to becoming a more courageous speaker.

Points to Ponder

1. Keep a log of the communications you have with others over the course of one day. What similarities to public speaking do you see in these interactions—whether face-to-face or mediated through technology?

2. Build on the list of positive outcomes of public speaking outlined in Chapter 18. What will go *right* when *you* speak?

3. In what ways do your expectations about public speaking serve you? In what ways might they work against you? Given the interplay of your talents and limitations, what realistic goals can you set for yourself as a speaker?

4. Create a list of your concerns about public speaking. While in a relaxed state, move through these imagined fears in your mind, one by one, until they lose their charge.

5. Recall a time when your perception of a situation was distorted. What factors contributed to your perception? How were you able to see the situation from a more realistic angle? Could this same dynamic be at work in your perceptions about public address? How so?

6. Revisit the step-by-step process for working through fears about public speaking described in Chapter 22. Apply this process to your next presentation.

7. In the sentence-completion exercises in Chapter 23, what recurring themes did you find in your set of fears and solutions? What potential strategies were you able to identify to enact these solutions?

8. Act on the advice in Chapter 24 and rehearse your speech in front of a live practice audience. What did you learn about your fears? Did this rehearsal help relieve any of your fears going forward?

9. Identify a minor decision that you feel in conflict about and use "chairwork" as outlined in Chapter 25. What came up for you? Were you surprised? When you feel comfortable with the process, explore any resistance that you might have about speaking in public.

10. Do you believe you are an introverted person? What strengths might this orientation give you? What challenges? (If unsure of your personality type, schools often offer the Myers-Briggs Type Indicator® at no or low cost and you can find free versions of the test online.)

11. Discuss one of your anxieties about public speaking with a trusted friend, relative, or classmate. Has this person ever experienced similar concerns? Did talking through your fear help you? How?

IV

MANAGING CONTENT

SUMMARY

Whether in ancient or modern times, a speaker selects, shapes, arranges, recalls, and presents ideas to a group. Choose and research topics that are meaningful and exciting to you, but be sure to offer your unique perspectives on the subject as well. You are the bridge that joins together listeners and topic, so take the time to choose your words wisely and craft each idea with care. The strategies that you use when constructing a speech will also help you manage your anxiety when delivering a speech. Organizational patterns, memory tools, visual aids, and mental rehearsal help build confidence you can lean on during your presentation.

Points to Ponder

1. Create a list of topics that have great meaning to you and that you would be excited to share with others. What opportunities do you have to speak about these topics in your classroom, workplace, or community?

2. What personal stories and insights can you share to create a unique slant on the list of topics you have just generated? Why might an audience find these perspectives valuable?

3. Reflect on some famous sayings and quotations. What makes them memorable? Did the speakers or writers of these words use any special techniques (assonance, alliteration, consonance, near rhyme, onomatopoeia)?

4. Consider Chapter 31's advice to craft ideas that are accurate, clear, original, on-point, and engaging. Are any of these tasks challenging for you? How might you improve your skills? Can you think of a writer or public speaker who could serve as a role model for you?

5. Choose a potential speech topic. How could you create an attention-getting opening and a memorable closing for this topic?

6. What does the word *extemporaneous* mean to you? Have you ever made a presentation speaking extemporaneously? How did you benefit from this style of presenting? How did your audience benefit?

7. Create a brief one-to-two-minute practice talk and use two of the memory tools offered in Chapter 34. In what ways did these techniques help you?

8. Recall your past experiences watching speakers use visual aids in a presentation. What worked well? Were there any mishaps? What can you learn from their successes and failures?

9. Have you ever used mental rehearsal to prepare for an event or performance? How can it help you when you prepare and deliver a speech?

V

STEPPING ONTO THE PODIUM

SUMMARY

Many of us feel self-conscious when we stand before a crowd. If we turn our attention inward and dwell on details the audience might perceive as imperfect, our anxiety will soar through the roof. On the other hand, if you apply a series of simple strategies both your message and manner will remain steadfast: dress comfortably for the occasion, breathe deeply and evenly, find or imagine friendly faces in the crowd, focus on the needs of the audience, attend only to the task at hand, and let your body, voice, and words project the same message. No matter how challenging the topic, audience, or occasion, when you stay connected with yourself, your material, and your listeners, stepping onto the podium can be an exhilarating experience.

Points to Ponder

1. When you are in an audience, what empathetic or encouraging thoughts do you feel towards the speaker? Imagine

and write down five kind thoughts that audience members will have towards you when you speak.

2. Consider asking classmates or coworkers to provide nonverbal support such as smiling while you speak. In addition, imagine friends, family members, and others in your life, past or present, who might serve as friendly faces in your mind during a speech. Does enlisting this aid help you to feel more confident? Why or why not?

3. Research Maslow's Hierarchy of Needs online or in a book. How can you keep these diverse audience needs in mind when selecting a topic and preparing and delivering a talk?

4. Keep a log of your conversations for one day and note what your verbal, vocal, and physical channels of communication seem to say during each interaction. Do listeners respond differently when these channels compliment or contradict one another?

5. Practice deep breathing while in a crowded area such as an airport, restaurant, concert, or sporting event. Do you notice a difference from how you might ordinarily feel? What other helpful techniques have you used to calm yourself during stressful situations?

6. Do you engage in enjoyable activities where you get lost in the moment and lose your sense of time? What steps can you take to invite this present-moment focus while speaking to a group?

7. Identify notables—whether politicians, entertainers, or business and civic leaders—whose clothing choices seem appropriate when presenting. What principles do they follow? Now, look through your own wardrobe. What clothing would work for you when presenting? What clothing might work against you? Why?

8. Reflect on the public speaking advice that you might have heard before reading Chapter 44. Which advice would you now consider "second-rate"? Which advice is still sound?

9. Have you ever watched a presentation in which the speaker was heckled or the audience became disruptive? How did the speaker handle it? What appropriate techniques would you use if your emotions or the audience threaten to get out of hand?

10. Identify three historical figures who championed unpopular views that are now widely accepted. How did they cope with adversity? How can you prepare yourself both cognitively and emotionally when you need to present a controversial point of view?

VI

STEPPING DOWN AND LOOKING BACK

SUMMARY

With your speech behind you, a new concern emerges: How did I do? Video recordings, audience feedback, and our own memories are important mirrors that help us assess our performances. Each of these mirrors has flaws, however, so learning to give ourselves approval is a critical task for speakers. In truth, no speaker is perfect. We speak to share a message, not to put on a flawless performance. Keeping this reality in mind will help you to feel confident at the podium, do your best, and improve from speech to speech.

Points to Ponder

1. Reflect on your public speaking journey thus far. What are you most proud of, to date? In what ways have you pleasantly surprised yourself?

2. Rehearse your speech in front of a practice audience and have a member film you. Ask the audience to assess your

message and delivery skills. How do your own recollections, the video recording, and audience responses differ? How are they alike?

3. Can you recall a speaker whose flaws worked instead as strengths? How could your own shortcomings be turned into assets?

4. Find an example of a famous speech that was not well received at the time. Would it have been wise for the speaker to judge his or her success by the reactions of the audience or the public? Why or why not?

VII

THE BIG PICTURE

SUMMARY

When we step back and look at the big picture, the highest purpose of public speaking looms clearly: to inspire our personal and collective growth. Whether spurred on by others or stirred by a deeper calling, be confident about the unique perspectives that you feel moved to share. Don't let naysayers dampen your voice or courage. Although not always embraced in the moment by an audience, we each carry valuable messages within. All speakers are, in fact, messengers. Speakers from one time and place often share messages that are valued in all times and all places. The voice of one can benefit the lives of many. You, too, can be such a voice.

Points to Ponder

1. Identify three past or present speakers who have inspired lasting change in the world. What topics could you speak about that might change someone's world?

2. Think of a person or group that you would like to honor in a speech. Why are they worthy of your admiration? How might dedicating your talk to this person or group inspire your best work in each facet of speechmaking?

3. What lasting thoughts or ideas have those from the past left with you? Why do you think those thoughts are so powerful and enduring? In what subtle or obvious ways might your own communications affect those around you?

4. Reflect on what inspires you in life. How could this inspiration help you as a speaker? What wisdom might you share with an audience?

5. What does it mean to prepare like it matters and relax as if it doesn't matter? What are some ways you can do this while crafting and presenting your speech?

6. Think of an activity you now do with ease that once scared you as a child. Has a similar shift occurred for you regarding public speaking? If not, can you imagine that it will happen given your inevitable growth as a person?

7. Reflect on the ways that life is like a speech, presented in Chapter 56. Which ways speak the most to you? How can you use these perspectives to become more confident both at the podium and in life?

USING *SPEAK WITH COURAGE*

CORRELATING THE 50+ TIPS WITH THE TOPICS OF YOUR COURSE

The handy table below will help you to find tips that augment topics you might cover in class. Organized in chronological fashion, these unique perspectives can enhance a speaker's confidence at any step of the speechmaking process. Sometimes this helpful advice is the main thrust of a chapter; sometimes you will find a tip nestled within a relevant passage or paragraph in a chapter. Because of their versatility, many tips appear in several categories.

Introduction to Public Speaking	1. Fear of Public Speaking Is Commonplace
	2. Even the Famous Get Scared
	3. Great Fear Can Precede Great Growth
	4. Indulge Your Self-Interest
	5. Big Brother Isn't Watching You
	17. Rethink How You Think about Speaking

ENDNOTES

Section I

1. The DSM-5 is the official source of professional guidelines used in the diagnosis and treatment of mental disorders. Quoted material appears on pages 198 and 199 of the *Diagnostic and Statistical Manual of Mental Disorders,* Fifth Edition: DSM-5 (Washington, D.C.: American Psychiatric Publishing, 2013).

2. It's no surprise that people fear heights, snakes, or public speaking. The extent and depth of the latter fear, however, is surprising. The *Bruskin Report*—published in July 1973 by R.H. Bruskin Associates of New Brunswick, New Jersey—first popularized the notion that Americans fear public speaking more than death. Speech professor Eric Metcalf's article "Speaking Publicly for Those Who, for Whatever Reason, Can't or Won't" (*Borough of Manhattan Community College Inquirer,* Fall 2007, Vol. 14) notes that "Number 53 was titled, 'What Are Americans Afraid of?'" Metcalf goes on to write, "To my knowledge no library in the world holds a copy." In 1977 the *Book of Lists* by Wallechinsky, Wallace, and Wallace further popularized the results of the Bruskin survey of over three thousand Americans. In May 2007, a survey of British supervisors conducted by the Aziz Corporation, a communications consulting firm, produced similar findings. In October 2008, Australia's leading public opinion research company, Newspoll, found that citizens down under fear public speaking more than death, too. Finally, M. Burnley, P. Cross, and N. Spanos published an article in the journal *Imagination, Cognition, and Personality* (1993) noting that up to 85 percent of Americans fear speaking in public. Anecdotally, each person to whom I mention *Speak with Courage* has a stage fright story of his or her own, too.

3. Quoted in Marianne Williamson, *A Return to Love: Reflections on the Principles of A COURSE IN MIRACLES* (New York: HarperOne, 2012), 190. The original

version of *A Return to Love* was published in 1992 by HarperCollins; the first HarperOne version was released in 2012.

4. The five notables mentioned in this passage appear in Frank Newport, "Mother Teresa Voted by American People as Most Admired Person of the Century," *Gallup News Service*, December 31, 1999, http://www.gallup.com/poll/3367/Mother -Teresa-Voted-American-People-Most-Admired-Person-Century.aspx. This Gallup survey took place from December 20–21, 1999. The ranking was not a compilation of previous surveys but rather a fresh listing based on the December 20–21 poll.

Section II

1. Several surveys show that a large percentage of Americans are or die intestate. *Consumer Reports* points out this high rate in its June 2005 issue and in a review of do-it-yourself last will and testament software in the November 10, 2011, edition of *Consumer Reports News*. An older Gallup poll from June 7, 2005, puts the figure for intestate Americans at 50 percent. Only 37 percent of those under age fifty had a will in that Gallup survey. Whether every other or two out of three Americans are intestate, the statistics remain telling. Perhaps the dynamic behind putting off wills and speaking in public is similar.

2. Dr. Donald McCabe of Rutgers University is a leading expert on academic integrity in America's high schools and colleges. McCabe conducts anonymous nationwide surveys in which he polls students about their academic habits. In a May 27, 2010, article, "Students' Cheating Takes a High-Tech Turn," Jeremy P. Meyer of the *Denver Post* wrote, "In his survey of 24,000 students at 70 high schools, 64 percent of students admitted to cheating on a test, 58 percent admitted to plagiarism and 95 percent said they participated in some form of cheating, whether it was on a test, plagiarism or copying homework." For additional information about professor McCabe's research, see the articles on this Rutgers University Web page: http://www.business.rutgers.edu/tags/332?page=1.

3. For a discussion on the quality of group decision making, see any edition of *Working in Groups* by Isa N. Engleberg and Dianna R. Wynn. When supporting claims about the quality of group decisions, these communication experts also refer to J. R. Katzenbach and D. K. Smith, *The Wisdom of Teams: Creating the High-Performance Organization* (New York: HarperBusiness, 1993).

4. Both sportswriters and sports websites report on home-field winning percentages in baseball and other professional sports. Although you wouldn't expect a scientific journal such as *Weather, Climate, and Society*, a quarterly journal of the American Meteorological Society, to shed light on home-field advantage in baseball, an article by Wes P. Kent and Scott C. Sheridan, "The Impact of Cloud Cover on Major League Baseball" (Vol. 3, Issue 1, January 2011), did just that. Leveling the playing field by eliminating eleven other variables, Kent and Sheridan's analysis of over 35,000 games found that home teams won "56% of the games played under clear skies compared to 52.3% of the games played under cloudy skies." Sunny skies or not, home teams win more often. Home-field advantage occurs in

other professional sports, too. Tobias Moskowitz and Jon Wertheim, in *Scorecasting* (New York: Three Rivers Press, 2011), note that games won by home teams range from 53.9% in Major League Baseball to 69.1% in Major League Soccer.

5. Since our skin is the body's largest organ, it's no surprise that activities such as massage, hot-tubbing, or hydrotherapy exert a calming influence over us. For a clinical study on the effects of hydrotherapy, see Jerrold Petrofsky et al., "The Influence of Warm Water Hydrotherapy on Muscle Relaxation" (Loma Linda University, 2003). Dr. Petrofsky, the lead researcher, is a professor of physical therapy at Loma Linda University.

6. When students ask "What's next?" after completing the basic public speaking course, I recommend our college's advanced public speaking course if it is offered. Next, I recommend joining a local chapter of Toastmasters International. According to their website, "Toastmasters International is a non-profit educational organization that teaches public speaking and leadership skills through a worldwide network of meeting locations" (http://www.toastmasters .org/Members/MembersFunctionalCategories/AboutTI.aspx). The organization currently boasts 14,350 clubs in 122 countries. While in graduate school, I participated in a local Toastmasters club and enjoyed the collegial, peer-to-peer training experience. Dale Carnegie also offers training seminars in effective presentations and other business skills.

Section III

1. The shift in thinking about public speaking is reflected in Steven A. Beebe, Susan J. Beebe, and Diana K. Ivy, *Communication Principles for a Lifetime, Volume 4: Presentational Speaking* (New York: Pearson Education, Inc., 2009).

2. For statistics about the frequency of text messages, see Aaron Smith, "Americans and Text Messaging," Pew Internet and American Life Project, September 19, 2011, http://www.pewinternet.org/Reports/2011/Cell-Phone-Texting-2011/Summary -of-Findings.aspx.

3. Author George Behe investigated and at times debunked 135 claimed cases of passenger and non-passenger premonitions in *Titanic: Psychic Forewarnings of a Tragedy* (Wellingsborough, England: The Acquarian Press, 1988). The story of Stephen Jenkin appears on page 134.

4. Although dictionaries commonly list "extrovert" as the preferred spelling for this personality trait, "extravert" is used by the Myers & Briggs Foundation and other professionals who work with the Myers-Briggs Type Indicator® (MBTI). The term "extravert" denotes a more complex psychological portrait than its plebian counterpart "extrovert" (see http://www.myersbriggs.org).

5. For a discussion of high IQ test scores among introverts, see Linda Silverman, "Introversion and Giftedness," Institute for the Study of Advanced Development, http://www.gifteddevelopment.com/Articles/counseling/c130.pdf. Dr. Silverman, also the author of *Giftedness 101* (New York: Springer Publishing, 2012), notes that giftedness and introversion share a positive correlation in that three times as many introverts have IQs above 160 in some research.

Section IV

1. The Duke Twins Study of Memory in Aging began in 1989. The Alzheimer's statistic noted in this chapter stems from an analysis of the National Academy of Science–National Research Council (NAS-NRC) Registry of Male World War II Veterans used in the Duke University study (http://aging-memory.duhs.duke.edu/twins.html). For a study comparing genetic and environmental influences on the personality traits of twins, see Auke Tellegen et al., "Personality Similarity in Twins Reared Apart and Together," *Journal of Personality and Social Psychology*, Vol. 54, no. 6 (1988): 1031–39.

2. Literacy and numeracy have been declining among American students for some time. See "Like Whatever," *Utne Reader* (July–August 2000): 28–29, and "Reading at Risk: A Survey of Literary Reading in America," Washington, D.C., National Endowment for the Arts (NEA) Research Division Report #46 (2004). Estimates of the number of words in current American English usage spring from the Google Ngram Viewer, a joint project with Harvard University. For further information about this fascinating linguistic tool, see Carolyn Y. Johnson, "In Billions of Words, Digital Allies Find Tale," *Boston Globe*, http://www.boston.com/news/science/articles/2010/12/17/harvard_google_join_in_study_of_books_from_past_200_years/.

3. College textbooks covering electronic research often distinguish between the "visible" and "deep" or "invisible" Web. Although these titles sound cryptic, put simply, they mean that popular search engines cannot access or display certain Web pages. School libraries, for example, pay for subscriptions to databases such as Academic Search Premier, so these results aren't available to search engines that pay no subscriber fees. A college reference librarian once told me that only 2 percent of available Internet search results appear through popular search engines; the other 98 percent reside in the "invisible" Web. For more information, see http://www.lib.berkeley.edu/TeachingLib/Guides/Internet/InvisibleWeb.html.

4. A form of supporting material as old as human history itself, stories—whether brief anecdotes or longer illustrations—engage, instruct, and endure in the memory of listeners. For a discussion of the power of stories in public speaking, see Isa N. Engleberg and John A. Daly, *Presentations in Everyday Life,* Second Edition (New York: Houghton Mifflin Company, 2005), 297–304.

5. The initial study at Brookdale Community College was conducted by me between 2003 and 2007 and summarized in a presentation: Martin McDermott, "The Four Horsemen of the Apocalypse: Unhorsing the Most Common Fears That Student Speakers Face," Great Ideas for Teaching Speech, Session #2, National Communication Association, Chicago, Illinois (November 17, 2007). Since 2007, I've continued the same classroom exercise and the results have been the same with more than a thousand additional students. The Canadian study by Murray B. Stein, John R. Walker, and David R. Forde surveyed nearly five hundred residents of Winnipeg, Manitoba. Their findings appear in "Public-Speaking Fears in a Community Sample: Prevalence, Impact on Functioning, and Diagnostic Classification," *Archives of General Psychiatry* 53, no. 2 (1996): 169–74.

6. Without the aid of PowerPoint and teleprompters, ancient Greek and Roman orators prized memory more highly than modern presenters. Cicero's five canons of rhetoric, in fact, included invention, arrangement, style, *memory*, and delivery. For a practical overview of memory systems—including those used by public speakers—see Harry Lorayne and Jerry Lucas, *The Memory Book* (New York: Random House, 1974).

Section V

1. For a full discussion of the study results, see Tom W. Smith, "Altruism in Contemporary America: A Report from the National Altruism Study," National Opinion Research Center, University of Chicago, July 25, 2003, http://www-news .uchicago.edu/releases/03/altruism.pdf.

2. The research of Dr. Albert Mehrabian, Professor Emeritus of Psychology, UCLA, is often taken out of context and generalized. The notion of a high reliance on nonverbal cues to decipher a speaker's meaning stems from two experiments that Mehrabian conducted in 1967. These experiments addressed incongruent verbal and nonverbal messages. In one experiment, listeners heard a recorded speaker say a single word and were then shown a picture of that speaker displaying an inconsistent facial expression. In these cases, subjects not surprisingly relied more heavily on tone of voice to intuit the speaker's feelings or attitudes.

3. "Objects" of meditation are not limited to mantras or the breath. Various traditions anoint physical objects such as candles, statues, or mandalas as such, and even mindful movement can serve as a "walking" meditation. Contemplative meditation traditions also deem certain topics as appropriate for reflection.

Section VI

1. Quoted in Thomas Freiling, *Walking with Lincoln: Spiritual Strength from America's Favorite President* (Grand Rapids, Michigan: Revell, 2009), 159.

Section VII

1. Disney's "It's a Small World" theme song and exhibit in the 1964–65 New York World's Fair might have inspired studies to determine how small the modern human world really is. Psychologist Stanley Milgram's 1967 experiment involved 296 volunteers who sent packages from the Midwest to a stranger in Massachusetts (Stanley Milgram, "The Small-World Problem," *Psychology Today*, Vol. 2, 1967, 60–67). It took between five and seven people to complete this task. In April 2010, a study of over five billion Twitter interactions by Sysomos, a provider of social media monitoring tools, found an average separation of 4.67 steps between users (Alex Cheng, "Six Degrees of Separation, Twitter Style," http://www.sysomos .com/insidetwitter/sixdegrees/). Not to be outdone, a study released on November 21, 2011, by researchers at Facebook and the University of Milan found that 721 million Facebook users were connected by an average of 4.74 people (see the news release on CNN: http://www.cnn.com/2011/11/22/tech/social -media/facebook-six-degrees/). In short, recent studies have shrunk John Guare's six degrees of separation down to less than five.

2. The original symbol for the Red Cross Movement simply reversed the colors of the flag of Switzerland, the country where the first Geneva Convention was ratified. The use of a red crescent first emerged in Turkey and other Islamic countries in the late 1800s to broaden acceptance of the organization's work. Although additional symbols are currently under consideration by the International Red Cross and Red Crescent Movement, its humanitarian mission will remain unchanged.

3. The USA Triathlon study was released on October 25, 2012. Of the thirty-eight race deaths noted, thirty were due to sudden cardiac arrest (SCA) during the swim portion of an event. (See Lawrence Creswell, "Triathlon-Related Deaths—The Facts and What You Should Know," http://www.endurancecorner.com/Larry_Creswell/triathlon_death.) Dr. Creswell was the lead investigator of the USA Triathlon medical review panel.

4. Although actor Richard Harris was seventy when he portrayed Marcus Aurelius as an aging emperor in the film *Gladiator*, the Roman ruler actually died at fifty-nine. Marcus Aurelius's book *Meditations* has and continues to appear on many "best books" lists, including John Coleman, "11 Books Every Young Leader Must Read," *Harvard Business Review Blog Net,* October 11, 2012, http://blogs.hbr.org/2012/10/11-books-every-young-leader-mu/.

INDEX